MW00479933

MEMOIR & POEMS
of
PHILLIS WHEATLEY

A NATIVE
AMERICAN AND A SLAVE

First published in 1834

Read & Co.

Copyright © 2021 Ragged Hand

This edition is published by Ragged Hand,
an imprint of Read & Co.

This book is copyright and may not be reproduced or copied in any
way without the express permission of the publisher in writing.

British Library Cataloguing-in-Publication Data
A catalogue record for this book is available
from the British Library.

Read & Co. is part of Read Books Ltd.
For more information visit
www.readandcobooks.co.uk

Dedication

to

The Right Honorable,

THE COUNTESS OF HUNTINGDON,

The Following Poems
are Most Respectfully Inscribed by
Her Much Obliged, Very Humble,
and Devoted Servant,

PHILLIS WHEATLEY
BOSTON. JUNE 12, 1773.

CONTENTS

PHILLIS WHEATLEY
By L. Maria Child 9

TO THE PUBLIC. 17

PREFACE 19

MR. WHEATLEY'S LETTER TO THE PUBLISHER. 21

INTRODUCTION. 23

MEMOIR 27

LETTER FROM GEORGE WASHINGTON
TO PHILLIS 45

POEMS

TO MÆCENAS 51

ON VIRTUE. 53

ON BRING BROUGHT FROM AFRICA
TO AMERICA 54

TO THE UNIVERSITY OF CAMBRIDGE,
IN NEW-ENGLAND 55

TO THE KING'S MOST EXCELLENT MAJESTY
1768 57

ON THE DEATH OF THE REV. DR. SEWELL
1769 58

ON THE DEATH OF THE
REV. MR. GEORGE WHITEFIELD
1770 60

ON THE DEATH OF A YOUNG LADY OF
FIVE YEARS OF AGE 62

ON THE DEATH OF A YOUNG GENTLEMAN.......64

TO A LADY ON HER HUSBAND'S DEATH 65

GOLIATH OF GATH- 1 SAM. CHAP. 17TH............67

THOUGHTS ON THE WORKS OF PROVIDENCE 74

TO A LADY, ON THE DEATH OF
THREE RELATIONS 79

THOUGHTS ON THE WORKS OF PROVIDENCE 81

HYMN TO THE MORNING 83

HYMN TO THE EVENING.........................84

ISAIAH, 63D CHAP. 1ST AND 8TH VERSES............85

ON RECOLLECTION 87

ON IMAGINATION...............................89

A FUNERAL POEM ON THE DEATH OF
C***** E*****, AN INFANT OF TWELVE MONTHS....91

TO CAPTAIN H******D OF THE 65TH REGIMENT.....93

TO THE RIGHT HONORABLE WILLIAM,
EARL OF DARTMOUTH, HIS MAJESTY'S
PRINCIPAL SECRETARY OF STATE FOR
NORTH AMERICA, &C............................94

ODE TO NEPTUNE. ON MRS. W———'S
VOYAGE TO ENGLAND 96

TO A LADY, ON HER COMING TO NORTH
AMERICA WITH HER SON, FOR THE
RECOVERY OF HER HEALTH......................97

TO A LADY, ON HER REMARKABLE
PRESERVATION IN A HURRICANE, IN
NORTH CAROLINA 99

TO A LADY AND HER CHILDREN,
ON THE DEATH OF HER SON AND
THEIR BROTHER 101

TO A GENTLEMAN AND LADY, ON THE
DEATH OF THE LADY'S BROTHER AND
SISTER, AND A CHILD OF THE NAME OF
AVIS, AGED ONE YEAR. 103

ON THE DEATH OF DR. SAMUEL MARSHALL
1771 105

TO A GENTLEMAN, ON HIS VOYAGE TO
GREAT BRITAIN FOR THE RECOVERY OF
HIS HEALTH. 107

TO THE REV. DR. THOMAS AMORY,
ON READING HIS SERMONS ON DAILY
DEVOTION, IN WHICH THAT DUTY IS
RECOMMENDED AND ASSISTED. 109

ON THE DEATH OF J. C. AN INFANT. 111

AN HYMN TO HUMANITY, TO S. P. G. ESQ; 113

TO THE HONOURABLE T. H. ESQ;
ON THE DEATH OF HIS DAUGHTER. 116

NIOBE IN DISTRESS FOR HER CHILDREN
SLAIN BY APOLLO FROM OVID'S
METAMORPHOSES, BOOK VI. AND
FROM A VIEW OF THE PAINTING OF MR.
RICHARD WILSON. 118

TO S. M. A YOUNG AFRICAN PAINTER,
ON SEEING HIS WORKS 126

TO HIS HONOUR THE LIEUTENANT-
GOVERNOR ON THE DEATH OF HIS
LADY. MARCH 24, 1773 128

A FAREWEL TO AMERICA. TO MRS. S. W. 130

A REBUS, BY I. B. 134

AN ANSWER TO THE REBUS,
BY THE AUTHOR OF THESE POEMS 135

PHILLIS WHEATLEY

By L. Maria Child

Phillis Wheatley was born in Africa, and brought to Boston, Massachusetts, in the year 1761,—a little more than a hundred years ago. At that time the people in Massachusetts held slaves. The wife of Mr. John Wheatley of Boston had several slaves; but they were getting too old to be very active, and she wanted to purchase a young girl, whom she could train up in such a manner as to make her a good domestic. She went to the slave-market for that purpose, and there she saw a little girl with no other clothing than a piece of dirty, ragged carpeting tied round her. She looked as if her health was feeble,—probably owing to her sufferings in the slave-ship, and to the fact of her having no one to care for her after she landed. Mrs. Wheatley was a kind, religious woman; and though she considered the sickly look of the child an objection, there was something so gentle and modest in the expression of her dark countenance, that her heart was drawn toward her, and she bought her in preference to several others who looked more robust. She took her home in her chaise, put her in a bath, and dressed her in clean clothes. They could not at first understand her; for she spoke an African dialect, sprinkled with a few words of broken English; and when she could not make herself understood, she resorted to a variety of gestures and signs. She did not know her own age, but, from her shedding her front teeth at that time, she was supposed to be about seven years old. She could not tell how long it was since the slave-traders tore her from her parents, nor where she had been since that time. The poor little orphan had probably

9

gone through so much suffering and terror, and been so unable to make herself understood by anybody, that her mind had become bewildered concerning the past. She soon learned to speak English; but she could remember nothing about Africa, except that she used to see her mother pour out water before the rising sun. Almost all the ancient nations of the world supposed that a Great Spirit had his dwelling in the sun, and they worshipped that Spirit in various forms. One of the most common modes of worship was to pour out water, or wine, at the rising of the sun, and to utter a brief prayer to the Spirit of that glorious luminary. Probably this ancient custom had been handed down, age after age, in Africa, and in that fashion the untaught mother of little Phillis continued to worship the god of her ancestors. The sight of the great splendid orb, coming she knew not whence, rising apparently out of the hills to make the whole world glorious with light, and the devout reverence with which her mother hailed its return every morning, might naturally impress the child's imagination so deeply, that she remembered it after she had forgotten everything else about her native land.

A wonderful change took place in the little forlorn stranger in the course of a year and a half. She not only learned to speak English correctly, but she was able to read fluently in any part of the Bible. She evidently possessed uncommon intelligence and a great desire for knowledge. She was often found trying to make letters with charcoal on the walls and fences. Mrs. Wheatley's daughter, perceiving her eagerness to learn, undertook to teach her to read and write. She found this an easy task, for her pupil learned with astonishing quickness. At the same time she showed such an amiable, affectionate disposition, that all members of the family became much attached to her. Her gratitude to her kind, motherly mistress was unbounded, and her greatest delight was to do anything to please her.

When she was about fourteen years old, she began to write poetry; and it was pretty good poetry, too. Owing to these uncommon manifestations of intelligence, and to the delicacy of her health, she was never put to hard household work, as was intended at the time of her purchase. She was kept constantly with Mrs. Wheatley and her daughter, employed in light and easy services for them. Her poetry attracted attention, and Mrs. Wheatley's friends lent her books, which she read with great eagerness. She soon acquired a good knowledge of geography, history, and English poetry; of the last she was particularly fond. After a while, they found she was trying to learn Latin, which she so far mastered as to be able to read it understandingly. There was no law in Massachusetts against slaves learning to read and write, as there have been in many of the States; and her mistress, so far from trying to hinder her, did everything to encourage her love of learning. She always called her affectionately, "My Phillis," and seemed to be as proud of her attainments as if she had been her own daughter. She even allowed her to have a fire and light in her own chamber in the evening, that she might study and write down her thoughts whenever they came to her.

Phillis was of a very religious turn of mind, and when she was about sixteen she joined the Orthodox Church, that worshipped in the Old-South Meeting-house in Boston. Her character and deportment were such that she was considered an ornament to the church. Clergymen and other literary persons who visited at Mrs. Wheatley's took a good deal of notice of her. Her poems were brought forward to be read to the company, and were often much praised. She was not unfrequently invited to the houses of wealthy and distinguished people, who liked to show her off as a kind of wonder. Most young girls would have had their heads completely turned by so much flattery and attention; but seriousness and humility seemed to be natural to Phillis. She always retained the same gentle, modest deportment that had won Mrs. Wheatley's heart when she first saw her in the slave-market. Sometimes, when she went abroad, she was invited to sit at table with other guests; but she always modestly declined, and requested that a plate might be placed for her on a side-table. Being well aware of the common prejudice against her complexion, she feared that some one might be offended by her company at their meals. By pursuing this course she manifested a natural politeness, which proved her to be more truly refined than any person could be who objected to sit beside her on account of her color.

Although she was tenderly cared for, and not required to do any fatiguing work, her constitution never recovered from the shock it had received in early childhood. When she was about nineteen years old, her health failed so rapidly that physicians said it was necessary for her to take a sea-voyage. A son of Mr. Wheatley's was going to England on commercial business, and his mother proposed that Phillis should go with him.

In England she received even more attention than had been bestowed upon her at home. Several of the nobility invited her to their houses; and her poems were published in a volume, with an engraved likeness of the author. In this picture she looks gentle and thoughtful, and the shape of her head denotes intellect. One of the engravings was sent to Mrs. Wheatley, who was delighted with it. When one of her relatives called, she pointed it out to her, and said, "Look at my Phillis! Does she not seem as if she would speak to me?"

Still the young poetess was not spoiled by flattery. One of the relatives of Mrs. Wheatley informs us, that "not all the attention she received, nor all the honors that were heaped upon her, had the slightest influence upon her temper and deportment. She was still the same single-hearted, unsophisticated being."

She addressed a poem to the Earl of Dartmouth, who was very kind to her during her visit to England.

Having expressed a hope for the overthrow of tyranny, she says:—

"Should you, my Lord, while you peruse my song,
Wonder from whence my love of Freedom sprung,—
Whence flow these wishes for the common good,
By feeling hearts alone best understood,—
I, young in life, by seeming cruel fate,
Was snatched from Afric's fancied happy state.
What pangs excruciating must molest,
What sorrows labor in my parent's breast!
Steeled was that soul, and by no misery moved,
That from a father seized his babe beloved.
Such was my case; and can I then but pray
Others may never feel tyrannic sway."

The English friends of Phillis wished to present her to their king, George the Third, who was soon expected in London. But letters from America informed her that her beloved benefactress, Mrs. Wheatley, was in declining health, and greatly desired to see her. No honors could divert her mind from the friend of her childhood. She returned to Boston immediately. The good lady died soon after; Mr. Wheatley soon followed; and the daughter, the kind instructress of her youth, did not long survive. The son married and settled in England. For a short time Phillis stayed with a friend of her deceased benefactress; then she hired a room and lived by herself. It was a sad change for her.

The war of the American Revolution broke out. In the autumn of 1776 General Washington had his head-quarters at Cambridge, Massachusetts; and the spirit moved Phillis to address some complimentary verses to him. . .

. . . The early friends of Phillis were dead, or scattered abroad, and she felt alone in the world. She formed an acquaintance with a colored man by the name of Peters, who kept a grocery shop. He was more than commonly intelligent, spoke fluently, wrote easily, dressed well, and was handsome in his person. He offered marriage, and in an evil hour she accepted him. He proved to be lazy, proud, and harsh-tempered. He neglected his business, failed, and became very poor. Though unwilling to do hard work himself, he wanted to make a drudge of his wife. Her constitution was frail, she had been unaccustomed to hardship, and she was the mother of three little children, with no one to help her in her household labors and cares. He had no pity on her, and instead of trying to lighten her load, he made it heavier by his bad temper. The little ones sickened and died, and their gentle mother was completely broken down by toil and sorrow. Some of the descendants of her lamented mistress at last heard of her illness and went to see her. They found her in a forlorn situation, suffering for the common comforts of life. The Revolutionary war was still raging. Everybody was mourning for sons and husbands slain in battle. The country was very poor.

The currency was so deranged that a goose cost forty dollars, and other articles in proportion. In such a state of things, people were too anxious and troubled to think about the African poetess, whom they had once delighted to honor; or if they transiently remembered her, they took it for granted that her husband provided for her. And so it happened that the gifted woman who had been patronized by wealthy Bostonians, and who had rolled through London in the splendid carriages of the English nobility, lay dying alone, in a cold, dirty, comfortless room. It was a mournful reverse of fortune; but she was patient and resigned. She made no complaint of her unfeeling husband; but the neighbors said that when a load of wood was sent to her, he felt himself too much of a gentleman to saw it, though his wife was shivering with cold. The descendants of Mrs. Wheatley did what they could to relieve her wants, after they discovered her extremely destitute condition; but, fortunately for her, she soon went "where the wicked cease from troubling, and where the weary are at rest."

Her husband was so generally disliked, that people never called her Mrs. Peters. She was always called Phillis Wheatley, the name bestowed upon her when she first entered the service of her benefactress, and by which she had become known as a poetess.

A CHAPTER FROM
The Freedmen's Book, 1865

TO THE PUBLIC

As it has been repeatedly suggested to the Publisher, by persons who have seen the Manuscript, that numbers would be ready to suspect they were not really the writings of Phillis, he has procured the following Attestation, from the most respectable characters in Boston, that none might have the least ground for disputing their original:

We, whose names are under-written, do assure the World, that the Poems specified in the following page[1] were (as we verily believe) written by Phillis, a young Negro girl, who was but a few years since brought an uncultivated barbarian from Africa, and has ever since been, and now is, under the disadvantage of serving as a slave in a family in this Town. She has been examined by some of the best judges, and is thought qualified to write them.

His Excellency, Thomas Hutchison, *Governor,*
The Hon. Andrew Oliver, *Lieutenant Governor,*

The Hon. Thomas Hubbard,
The Hon. John Erving,
The Hon. James Pitts,
The Hon. Harrison Gray,
The Hon. James Bowdoin,

---

1   The words 'following page' allude to the Contents of the Manuscript Copy, which are wrote at the back of the above Attestation.

John Hancock, Esq.
Joseph Green, Esq.
Richard Carey, Esq.,,

The Rev. Charles Chauncey, D.D.
The Rev. Matthew Byles, D.D.
The Rev. Edw'd Pemberton, D.D.
The Rev. Andrew Elliot, D.D.
The Rev. Samuel Cooper, D.D.
The Rev. Mr. Samuel Mather,
The Rev. Mr. John Moorhead,
Mr. John Wheatley, (her Master.),

N.B. The original Attestation, signed by the above Gentlemen, may be seen by applying to Archibald Bell, Bookseller, No. 8, Aldgate Street.

PREFACE

The following Poems were written originally for the amusement of the Author, as they were the products of her leisure moments. She had no intention ever to have published them; nor would they now have made their appearance, but at the importunity of many of her best and most generous friends, to whom she considers herself as under the greatest obligation.

As her attempts in Poetry are now sent into the world, it is hoped the critic will not severely censure their defects; and we presume they have too much merit to be cast aside as worthless and trifling effusions. As to the disadvantages she has labored under, with regard to learning, nothing needs to be offered, as her master's letter, which follows, will sufficiently show the difficulties in this respect she had to encounter.

With all their imperfections, the Poems are now humbly submitted to the perusal of the Public.

MR. WHEATLEY'S
LETTER TO THE PUBLISHER

The following is a copy of a Letter sent by the Author's Master to the publisher:—

Phillis was brought from Africa to America in the year 1761, between seven and eight years of age. Without any assistance from school education, and by only what she was taught in the family, she, in sixteen months' time from her arrival, attained the English language, to which she was an utter stranger before, to such a degree as to read any, the most difficult parts of the Sacred Writings, to the great astonishment of all who heard her.

As to her writing, her own curiosity led her to it; and this she learned in so short a time, that in the year 1765 she wrote a letter to the Rev. Mr. Occum, the Indian minister, while in England.

She has a great inclination to learn the Latin Tongue, and has made some progress in it.

This relation is given by her Master, who bought her, and with whom she now lives.

JOHN WHEATLEY,
Boston, Nov. 14, 1772.

INTRODUCTION

Sketches of the lives of those who have been distinguished for talents and virtues, are generally acknowledged to have a happy moral influence. But especially is it the case, that, when these qualities have raised the individual who possesses them from the humblest walks of life, to the notice and approbation of the wise and good in its elevated stations, the example cannot but be an encouragement and a gratification to those gifted spirits, unto whom the lines have fallen in the shade-places of life, but who aspire to pitch their tent in the sunshine.

Under these impressions, we introduce to the reader the subject of the following Memoir, whom we find in the lowest condition of humanity; for she was sold and bought like a beast in the market! and that in the same land where, shortly after, the people rose in their indignation against oppression, and asserted, in the face of a frowning world, that 'All men are born free and equal.'

But the stain of slavery has long been erased from the annals of New-England. The groan of the African is not heard among her beautiful hills, nor the whip of the task-master in her pleasant valleys. Would it were thus unto our farthest shores! How can a free people be a slave-holding people? Surely in that social community, where man is claimed as the property of his fellow, the corner-stone of the Temple of Liberty must be laid in the sand; and whither shall we flee when such frail foundation is unsettled?

We have been told of the happiness of the Negro in his bondage; how blithely he joins in the dance, and how joyously he lifts the burthen of the song, and how free he is from all care for the morrow. But would the free man change places with the slave? Does he envy his condition? It was said of the peasants of France, in the days of a stern master, that they danced to forget their servitude. Mere animal excitement is the enjoyment of the beasts of the forest and the field, the bird of the air, the fish of the sea, and the million insect tribes, sporting in every sun-beam; but this is not the happiness of man. This has to do with mind, and that mind possesses the greatest capacities for happiness, which is most developed, enlarged and improved. How, then, can it be said that the poor slave is happy, whose soul is bound down to the dust by the chains of ignorance and sin? Does his master say he will instruct him? he will teach him? He cannot. He dare not. Let the coffers of science be unlocked to the African. Give him free access to the treasures of knowledge. Make him acquainted with the wealth of his own spirit—his own strength—and his own rights—and the white man would strive to bind him as vainly as the Philistines strove against Sampson. Even now, in his day of darkness, how often has he made the hearts of his keepers to quail, and their cheeks to blanch with fear, when they have looked on their wives and little ones, and heard the cry of vengeance fill their plantations with dismay.

But even were the thrall of bondage broken, the hapless victim of slavery would find himself, in but too many cases, we fear, fettered by prejudice—despised by the proud—insulted by the scornful. Such has been another of the poisonous operations of slavery on public sentiment. But we are not about to weary the reader with the horrors of this system. It will be our humble endeavor, simply to present an unvarnished record of African genius, sustained by Christian benevolence, and guided by Christian faith.

We will not, however, conclude our remarks, without reference to that spirit of the present time which manifestly is moving abroad on the face of society, for the amelioration of the condition, and the development of the capacity of the African, of every class. We are glad to perceive that serious and strenuous efforts are being made for the benefit of some of our States—

where this system is in its strong-holds—at the suggestion of good men, for the religious instruction of the slaves. There cannot be the least doubt, as it seems to us, that this measure is not only safe and seasonable, but that the policy of the master, so long as he remains a master, requires it not less than the true happiness of the slave. But especially is it desirable, among the preparations to the great work of general emancipation, which we trust is not only borne in mind constantly by all good men, but is not far distant in reality. In a word, all the exertions now made, by the benevolent friends of the African, appear to us likely to produce or suggest, directly or indirectly, a great amount of good, and to promise the early dawning of that bright day, when, in the moral view of his fellow men, no less than of that Creator who has 'made them all of one blood,' the African shall be as the American, and the black man as the white.

MEMOIR

Phillis Wheatley was a native of Africa; and was brought to this country in the year 1761, and sold as a slave.

She was purchased by Mr. John Wheatley, a respectable citizen of Boston. This gentleman, at the time of the purchase, was already the owner of several slaves; but the females in his possession were getting something beyond the active periods of life, and Mrs. Wheatley wished to obtain a young negress, with the view of training her up under her own eye, that she might, by gentle usage, secure to herself a faithful domestic in her old age. She visited the slave-market, that she might make a personal selection from the group of unfortunates offered for sale. There she found several robust, healthy females, exhibited at the same time with Phillis, who was of a slender frame, and evidently suffering from change of climate. She was, however, the choice of the lady, who acknowledged herself influenced to this decision by the humble and modest demeanor and the interesting features of the little stranger.

The poor, naked child (for she had no other covering than a quantity of dirty carpet about her, like a 'fillibeg') was taken home in the chaise of her mistress, and comfortably attired. She is supposed to have been about seven years old, at this time, from the circumstance of shedding her front teeth. She soon gave indications of uncommon intelligence, and was frequently seen endeavoring to make letters upon the wall with a piece of chalk or charcoal.

A daughter[2] of Mrs. Wheatley, not long after the child's first introduction to the family, undertook to learn her to read and

2   This lady was better known subsequently as Mrs. Lothrop.

write; and, while she astonished her instructress by her rapid progress, she won the good-will of her kind mistress, by her amiable disposition and the propriety of her behaviour. She was not devoted to menial occupations, as was at first intended; nor was she allowed to associate with the other domestics of the family, who were of her own color and condition, but was kept constantly about the person of her mistress.

She does not seem to have preserved any remembrance of the place of her nativity, or of her parents, excepting the simple circumstance that her mother *poured out water before the sun at his rising*—in reference, no doubt, to an ancient African custom. The memories of most children reach back to a much earlier period than their seventh year; but there are some circumstances (that will shortly appear) which would induce us to suppose, that in the case of Phillis, this faculty did not equal the other powers of her mind. Should we be mistaken in this inference, the faithlessness of memory, concerning the scenes of her childhood, may be otherwise accounted for.

We cannot know at how early a period she was beguiled from the hut of her mother; or how long a time elapsed between her abduction from her first home and her being transferred to the abode of her benevolent mistress, where she must have felt like one awaking from a fearful dream. This interval was, no doubt, a long one; and filled, as it must have been, with various degrees and kinds of suffering, might naturally enough obliterate the recollection of earlier and happier days. The solitary exception which held its place so tenaciously in her mind, was probably renewed from day to day through this long season of affliction; for, every morning, when the bereaved child saw the sun emerging from the wide waters, she must have thought of her mother, prostrating herself before the first golden beam that glanced across her native plains.

As Phillis increased in years, the development of her mind realized the promise of her childhood; and she soon attracted the attention of the literati of the day, many of whom furnished her with books. These enabled her to make considerable progress in belles-lettres; but such gratification seems only to have increased her thirst after knowledge, as is the case with most gifted minds, not misled by vanity; and we soon find her endeavoring to master the Latin tongue.

She was now frequently visited by clergymen, and other individuals of high standing in society; but notwithstanding the attention she received, and the distinction with which she was treated, she never for a moment lost sight of that modest, unassuming demeanor, which first won the heart of her mistress in the slave-market. Indeed, we consider the strongest proof of her worth to have been the earnest affection of this excellent woman, who admitted her to her own board. Phillis ate of her bread, and drank of her cup, and was to her as a daughter; for she returned her affection with unbounded gratitude, and was so devoted to her interests as to have no will in opposition to that of her benefactress.

We cannot ascertain that she ever received any formal manumission; but the chains which bound her to her master and mistress were the golden links of love, and the silken bands of gratitude. She had a child's place in their house and in their hearts. Nor did she, notwithstanding their magnanimity in setting aside the prejudices against color and condition, when they found these adventitious circumstances dignified by talents and worth, ever presume on their indulgence either at home or abroad. Whenever she was invited to the houses of individuals of wealth and distinction, (which frequently happened,) she always declined the seat offered her at their board, and, requesting that a side-table might be laid for her, dined modestly apart from the rest of the company.

We consider this conduct both dignified and judicious. A woman of so much mind as Phillis possessed, could hot but be aware of the emptiness of many of the artificial distinctions of life. She could not, indeed, have felt so utterly unworthy to sit down among the guests, with those by whom she had been bidden to the banquet. But she must have been painfully conscious of the feelings with which her unfortunate race were regarded; and must have reflected that, in a mixed company, there might be many individuals who would, perhaps, think they honored her too far by dining with her at the same table. Therefore, by respecting even the prejudices of those who courteously waived them in her favor, she very delicately expressed her gratitude; and, following the counsels of those Scriptures to which she was not a stranger, by taking the lowest seat at the feast, she placed herself where she could certainly expect neither to give or receive offence.

It is related that, upon the occasion of one of these visits, the weather changed during the absence of Phillis; and her anxious mistress, fearful of the effects of cold and damp upon her already delicate health, ordered Prince (also an African and a slave) to take the chaise, and bring home her *protegee*. When the chaise returned, the good lady drew near the window, as it approached the house, and exclaimed—'Do but look at the saucy varlet—if he has'nt the impudence to sit upon the same seat with *my Phillis!* And poor Prince received a severe reprimand for forgetting the dignity thus kindly, though perhaps to him unaccountably, attached to the sable person of 'my Phillis.'

In 1770, at the age of sixteen, Phillis was received as a member of the church worshipping in the Old South Meeting House, then under the pastoral charge of the Rev. Dr. Sewall. She became an ornament to her profession; for she possessed that meekness of spirit, which, in the language of inspiration, is said to be above all price. She was very gentle-tempered, extremely affectionate, and altogether free from that most despicable foible, which might naturally have been her besetting sin—literary vanity.

The little poem commencing,

' 'T was mercy brought me from my heathen land,'

will be found to be a beautiful expression of her religious sentiments, and a noble vindication of the claims of her race. We can hardly suppose any one, reflecting by whom it was written—an African and a slave— to read it without emotions both of regret and admiration.

Phillis never indulged her muse in any fits of sullenness or caprice. She was at all times accessible. If any one requested her to write upon any particular subject or event, she immediately set herself to the task, and produced something upon the given theme. This is probably the reason why so many of her pieces are funeral poems, many of them, no doubt, being written at the request of friends. Still, the variety of her compositions afford sufficient proof of the versatility of her genius. We find her at one time occupied in the contemplation of an event affecting the condition of a whole people, and pouring forth her thoughts in a lofty strain. Then the song sinks to the soft tones of sympathy in the affliction occasioned by domestic bereavement. Again, we observe her seeking inspiration from the sacred volume, or from the tomes of heathen lore; now excited by the beauties of art, and now hymning the praises of nature to 'Nature's God.' On one occasion, we notice her—a girl of but fourteen years—recognizing a political event, and endeavoring to express the grateful loyalty of subjects to their rightful king—not as one, indeed, who had been trained to note the events of nations, by a course of historical studies, but one whose habits, taste and opinions, were peculiarly her own; for in Phillis we have an example of originality of no ordinary character. She was allowed, and even encouraged, to follow the leading of her own genius; but nothing was forced upon her, nothing suggested, or placed before her as a lure; her literary efforts were altogether the natural workings of her own mind.

There is another circumstance respecting her habits of composition, which peculiarly claims our attention. She did not seem to have the power of retaining the creations of her own fancy, for a long time, in her own mind. If, during the vigil of a wakeful night, she amused herself by weaving a tale, she knew nothing of it in the morning—it had vanished in the land of dreams. Her kind mistress indulged her with a light, and in the cold season with a fire, in her apartment, during the night. The light was placed upon a table at her bed-side, with writing materials, that if anything occurred to her after she had retired, she might, without rising or taking cold, secure the swift-winged fancy, ere it fled.

We have before remarked, that Mrs. Wheatley did not require or permit her services as a domestic; but she would sometimes allow her to polish a table or dust an apartment, (occupations which were not thought derogatory to the dignity of a lady in those days of primitive simplicity,) or engage in some other trifling occupation that would break in upon her sedentary habits; but not unfrequently, in these cases, the brush and the duster were soon dropped for the pen, that her meditated verse might not escape her.

It has been suggested that memory was in fault in this instance; but we have hesitated to account for this singular habit of mind in this manner; for, upon duly considering the point, we cannot suppose that Phillis could have made such rapid progress in various branches of knowledge, if she had not possessed a retentive memory—and still less, that she could have succeeded in the attainment of one of the dead languages. We are rather inclined to refer the fact in question to some peculiar structure of mind—possibly to its activity— perhaps occasioned by lack of early discipline—one fancy thrusting forth another, and occupying its place.

But the difficulty still remains, that she could not recall those fancies. Most persons are aware that, by a mental effort, (and there is no operation of the mind more wonderful) they can recall scenes and events long since forgotten; but Phillis does not seem to have possessed this power, as it respects her own productions,—for we believe this singularity to have affected her own thoughts only, and not the impressions made upon her mind by the thoughts of others, communicated by books or conversation.

We consider this statement of the case corroborated by the poem on 'Recollection.' In this little effusion, referring so directly to the point in question, we find no intimation or acknowledgment of any deficiency, but rather the contrary; and when we remember Phillis's simplicity of character, we cannot suppose that an imperfection of the kind would have been thus passed unnoticed, had any such existed. But, however this singularity may be accounted for, we state the fact as we believe it to have existed, and leave our readers to draw their own inferences. Perhaps there may be many gifted minds conscious of the same peculiarity.

By comparing the accounts we have of Phillis's progress, with the dates of her earliest poems, we find that she must have commenced her career as an authoress, as soon as she could write a legible hand, and without being acquainted with the rules of composition. Indeed, we very much doubt if she ever had any grammatical instruction, or any knowledge of the structure or idiom of the English language, except what she imbibed from a perusal of the best English writers, and from mingling in polite circles, where fortunately, she was encouraged to converse freely with the wise and the learned.

We gather from her writings, that she was acquainted with astronomy, ancient and modern geography, and ancient history; and that she was well versed in the scriptures of the Old and New Testament. She discovered a decided taste for the stories of Heathen Mythology, and Pope's Homer seems to have been a great favorite with her. Her time, when she was at home, was chiefly occupied with her books, her pen, and her needle; and when we consider the innocence of her life, the purity of her heart, and the modest pride which must have followed her successful industry, joined to the ease and contentment of her domestic lot, we cannot but suppose these early years to have been years of great happiness.

The reader is already aware of the delicate constitution and frail health of Phillis. During the winter of 1773, the indications of disease had so much increased, that her physician advised a sea voyage. This was earnestly seconded by her friends; and a son of Mr. and Mrs. Wheatley being about to make a voyage to England, to arrange a mercantile correspondence, it was settled that Phillis should accompany him, and she accordingly embarked in the summer of the same year.

She was at this time but nineteen years old, and was at the highest point of her short and brilliant career. It is with emotions of sorrow that we ap- proach the strange and splendid scenes which were now about to open upon her—to be succeeded by grief and desolation.

Phillis was well received in England, and was presented to Lady Huntingdon, Lord Dartmouth, Mr. Thornton,[3] and many other individuals of distinction; but, says our informant, 'not all the attention she received, nor all the honors that were heaped upon her, had the slightest influence upon her temper or deportment. She was still the same single-hearted, unsophisticated being.' During her stay in England, her poems were given to the world, dedicated to the Countess of Huntingdon, and embellished with an engraving which is said to have been a striking representation of the original. It is supposed that one of these impressions was forwarded to her mistress, as soon as they were struck off; for a grand-niece of Mrs. Wheatley's informs us that, during the absence of Phillis, she one day called upon her relative, who immediately directed her attention to a picture over the fireplace, exclaiming—'See! look at my Phillis! does she not seem as though she would speak to me!'

Phillis arrived in London so late in the season, that the great mart of fashion was deserted. She was therefore urgently pressed by her distinguished friends to remain until the Court

3   Another of the benefactors of Dartmouth College.

returned to St. James's, that she might be presented to the young monarch, George III. She would probably have consented to this arrangement, had not letters from America informed her of the declining health of her mistress, who entreated her to return, that she might once more behold her beloved protegee.

Phillis waited not a second bidding, but immediately re-embarked, and arrived in safety at that once happy home, which was so soon to be desolate. It will probably occur to the reader as singular, that Phillis has not borne a more decided testimony to the kindness of those excellent friends who so tenderly cherished her. Her farewell to America was inscribed to her mistress, indicated by the initials S. W., but here she merely alludes to the pain of parting. If any other pieces were ever devoted to her, they were doubtless destroyed; for, upon mentioning the singularity of her omitting to record a testimony of her gratitude to her benefactors, we are told, by one of the very few individuals who have any recollection of Mrs. Wheatley or Phillis, that the former was a woman distinguished for good sense and discretion; and that her Christian humility induced her to shrink from the thought of those good deeds being blazoned forth to the world, which were performed in the privacy of her own happy home. It appears, also, that on her death-bed she requested that nothing might be written upon her decease. Indeed, Phillis was forbidden this indulgence of her grief; and it was shortly after her mournful duty to close the eyes of her indulgent mistress and unwearied friend.

The decease of this excellent lady occurred in the year 1774. Her husband soon followed her to the house appointed for all living; and their daughter joined them in the chambers of death. The son had married and settled in England; and Phillis was now, therefore, left utterly desolate. She spent a short time with a friend of her departed mistress, and then took an apartment, and lived by herself. This was a strange change to one who had enjoyed the comforts and even luxuries of life, and the happiness of a fireside where a well regulated family were accustomed to gather. Poverty, too, was drawing near, with its countless afflictions. She could hope for little extraneous aid; the troubles with the mother country were thickening around; every home was darkened, and every heart was sad.

At this period of destitution, Phillis received an offer of marriage from a respectable colored man of Boston. The name of this individual was Peters. He kept a grocery in Court Street, and was a man of handsome person and manners; he wore a wig, carried a cane, and quite acted out *'the gentleman.'* In an evil hour he was accepted; and he proved utterly unworthy of the distinguished woman who honored him by her alliance. He was unsuccessful in business, and failed soon after their marriage; and he is said to have been both too proud and too indolent to apply himself to any occupation below his fancied dignity. Hence his unfortunate wife suffered much from this ill-omened union.

The difficulties between the colonies and the mother country had by this time increased to open hostilities. Universal distress prevailed. The provincial army was scantily provided with clothing and food; and the families of those who were fighting for their country, most of whom had been cherished in the lap of plenty, were glad to obtain their daily bread. The inhabitants of Boston were fleeing in all direction; and Phillis accompanied her husband to Wilmington, in this State. In an obscure country village, the necessaries of life are always obtained with more difficulty than in a populous town, and in this season of scarcity, Phillis suffered much from privation—from absolute want—and from painful exertions to which she was unaccustomed, and for which her frail constitution unfitted her. We cannot be surprised that, under these distressing circumstances, her health, which had been much improved by her voyage to England, should have again declined. We rather wonder, that one who had been so tenderly reared, and so fondly nurtured, should have borne up, for so long a season, against such an increasing burthen of misfortune and affliction.

In the course of these years of suffering, she became the mother of three infants, who inherited the frail health of their parent; and thus to her other cares was added the anxiety of a mother, watching the flickering flame glowing in the bosom of her offspring, and trembling every moment, lest the breath of adversity should extinguish a life so dear to her. We know little of Phillis in her relations of wife and mother; but we cannot suppose, that one who had been so faithful to her earliest friend, who was so meek and unassuming and possessed of such an affectionate constitutional disposition, could have been unmindful, in any case, of her conjugal or matronly duties. Nor can we learn that a breath of complaint or reproach ever escaped her respecting her husband. There are some, however, not so tender of a name she was not allowed to bear, who speak of him as that man deserves to be spoken of, who beguiles a woman to confide in his protection, and betrays her trust and his own.

We have alluded above to the circumstance that we never heard Phillis named, or alluded to, by any other appellation than that of 'Phillis Wheatley'—a name which she sustained with dignity and honor, not only in the vicinity of her own residence, but upon far distant shores. After the evacuation of Boston by the British troops, Phillis returned thither. A niece of Mrs. Wheatley's, whose son had been slain in battle, received her beneath her own roof. This lady was a widow, and not wealthy. She kept a small day school, to increase her narrow income. Her mansion had been much injured by the enemy, but it afforded a shelter to herself and daughter, and they ministered to Phillis, and her three suffering children, for six weeks. At the end of that period, Peters came for his wife, and, having provided an apartment, took her thither with her little family.

It must be remembered that this was a season of general poverty Phillis's friends of former days were scattered far and wide. Many of them, attached to the royal interest, had left the country. The successful patriots, during the seven-years' contention, had not only lost the profits which would have arisen from their industry, but were obliged to strain every nerve to meet the exigences of the war. The depreciation of the currency added greatly to the general distress. Mr. Thacher, for example, in his History of Plymouth, tells us of a man who sold a cow for forty dollars, and gave the same sum for a goose! We have ourselves heard an elderly lady[4] relate, that her husband, serving in the army, forwarded her in a letter fifty dollars, which was of so little value when she received it, that she paid the whole for a quarter of mutton, so poor and so tough, that it required, great skill and patience, in the culinary department, to render it fit for the table. 'In this condition of things,' observes the lady, whom we have more than once referred to, and to whom we expressed our surprise at the neglect and poverty into which Phillis was suffered to decline, 'people had other things to attend to than prose and poetry, and had little to bestow in charity, when their own children were clamorous for bread.' Poor Phillis was left to the care of her negligent husband.

We now learn nothing of her for a long interval. At length a relative of her lamented mistress heard of her illness, and sought her out. She was also visited by several other members of that family. They found her in a situation of extreme misery. Two of her children were dead, and the third was sick unto death. She was herself suffering for want of attention, for many comforts, and that greatest of all comforts in sickness— cleanliness. She was reduced to a condition too loathsome to describe. If a charitable individual, moved at the sight of so much distress, sent a load of wood, to render her more comfortable during the cold season, her husband *was too much of a gentleman* to prepare it for her use. It is painful to dwell upon the closing scene. In a filthy apartment, in an obscure part of the metropolis, lay the dying mother, and the wasting child. The woman who had stood honored and respected in the presence of the wise and good of that country which was hers by adoption, or rather compulsion,

---

4   The grandmother of the writer of this Memoir.

who had graced the ancient halls of Old England, and rolled about in the splendid equipages of the proud nobles of Britain, was now numbering the last hours of life in a state of the most abject misery, surrounded by all the emblems of squalid poverty!

Little more remains to be told. It is probable (as frequently happens when the constitution has long borne up against disease) that the thread of life, attenuated by suffering, at last snapped suddenly; for the friends of Phillis, who had visited her in her sickness, knew not of her death. Peters did not see fit to acquaint them with the event, or to notify them of her interment. A grand-niece of Phillis's benefactress, passing up Court Street, met the funeral of an adult and a child. A bystander informed her they were bearing Phillis Wheatley to that silent mansion 'where the wicked cease from troubling, and the weary are at rest.'

They laid her away in her solitary grave, without a stone to tell that one so good and so gifted sleeps beneath; and the waters of oblivion are rapidly erasing her name from the sands of time. We would that her memory were engraven upon the heart of the young and the gifted, who are striving for a niche in the temple of fame. We think, gentle reader, she is as worthy of a place in your thoughts, as the heroines of the thousand tales dressed out to beguile your fancy. Remember, that though the children of men regard feature and complexion, there is One who looketh upon the heart.

Here and there we find a solitary pilgrim, belonging to the days of the years that are gone, treasuring Phillis's poems as a precious relic. But when *they* shall have passed away, who will remember her? May not this little record, though offered with diffidence, be allowed to perpetuate her name?

The poems now republished, are as they came from the hands of the author, without the alteration of a word or letter. Surely they lift an eloquent voice in behalf of her race.

Is it urged that Phillis is but a solitary instance of African genius? Even though this were the case—which we by no means grant—we reply that, had Phillis fallen into less generous and affectionate hands, she would speedily have perished under the privations and exertions of common servitude. Or had she dragged out a few years of suffering, she would have been of much less value to her master than the sturdy negress of more obscure faculties, but whose stronger limbs could have borne heavier burthens. How then can it be known, among this unfortunate people, how often the light of genius is quenched in suffering and death? The great difference between the colored man and his oppressors seems to us to be, that the great Ruler of the universe has appointed power unto the white man for a season; and verily they have bowed down their brethren with a rod of iron. From the luxuriant savannahs of America, and the barren sands of Africa, the blood of their victims cries unto God from the ground.

Friends of liberty! friends of humanity! when will ye appoint a jubilee for the African, and let the oppressed go free?

We have named, in the course of the preceding Memoir, some of the remarkable privileges which fell to the lot of Phillis. We should allude also more distinctly to the general disadvantages of her condition. It must not be forgotten, that the opportunities of education allowed females, at this early period, were few and meagre. Those who coveted superior advantages for their children, sent them home (as the mother country was fondly termed) for their education. Of course, this expensive method could be adopted only by a privileged few, chiefly belonging to old English families of rank and wealth. The great mass of American females could boast of few accomplishments save housewifery. They had few books beside their Bibles. They were not expected to read—far less to write. It was their province to guide the spindle and distaff, and work willingly with their hands. Now, woman is allowed to establish her humble stool somewhat nearer the elbow-chair of her lord and master; to pore over the huge tome of science, hitherto considered as his exclusive property; to con the musty volumes of classic lore, written even in strange tongues; to form her own opinions, and give them forth to the world. But, in the days of Phillis, these things were not so. She was not stimulated to exertion by the successful cultivation of female talent. She had no brilliant exhibition of feminine genius before her, to excite her emulation; and we are at a loss to conjecture, how the first strivings of her mind after knowledge—her delight in literature, her success even in a dead language, the first bursting forth of her thoughts in song—can be accounted for, unless these efforts are allowed to have been the inspirations of that genius which is the gift of God. And who will dare to say, that the benevolent Sovereign of the universe has appointed her unfortunate race to be hewers of wood and drawers of water, and given them no portion with their brethren?

The distinguished women of France were trained, as it were, in the very temple of science, to minister at its altars. Those of England, stood, too, in the broad light of its wide-spreading beams; but at the time when Phillis lived, our own land was darkly over-shadowed. We had no philosophers, no historians, no poets; and our statesmen—those wonderful men, who stood forth in the day of a nation's peril, the wonder and glory of the world—had not then breathed forth those mighty energies which girded the warrior for the battle, and nerved the hearts of a whole people as the heart of one man. All here was calm and passionless as the natural world upon the morning of creation, ere the Spirit of God had moved upon the face of the waters. It passed, and the day-spring knew its place. Even thus with the Spirit of Liberty. It breathed upon our sleeping nation, awakening the genius of the people to appear from time to time in a thousand new and multiplying forms of ever-varying beauty.

Since that day, our philosophers have stood in the courts of monarchs, more honored than he who held the sceptre; and the recesses of the leafy forest, and the banks of the solitary stream and lonely lake, have been hallowed by the legends of the children of song. Nor has skill been wanting to embody the deeds of our fathers, or shadow forth the gentle and the brave, in tales that have stirred many hearts, even beyond the waters. But Phillis lived not amid these happy influences. True, she heard the alarum of Liberty, but it was in suffering and sorrow; and when the shout of triumph was raised, it fell upon a chilled heart and a closing ear. The pride of victory could scarce move the sympathies of one who had known the emptincss of glory, and proved the mockery of fame.

The evidences she has left us of her genius, were the productions of early and happy days, before her mind was matured by experience, the depths of her soul fathomed by suffering, or her fine powers chastened by affliction. The blight was upon her in her spring-time, and she passed away.

The reader may claim to be satisfied as to the authenticity of the facts stated in the preceding Memoir.

They were derived from grand-nieces of Phillis's benefactress, who are still living, and have a distinct and vivid remembrance both of their excellent relative and her admired protegee.

Their statements are corroborated by a grand-daughter of that lady, now residing in Boston; who, though much younger than the individuals alluded to, recollects the circumstance of Phillis's visiting at the house of her father. Other company was probably present; for the lady in question relates, that the domestics observed, 'it was the first time they ever carried tea to a colored woman.' This lady communicates some particulars which we state with great pleasure, as they remove from Phillis the supposition of her having formed a matrimonial connection from unworthy or mercinary motives. She assures us that Peters was not only a very remarkable looking man, but a man of talents and information; and that he wrote with fluency and propriety, and at one period read law. It is admitted, however, that he was disagreeable in his manners, and that on account of his improper conduct, Phillis became entirely estranged from the immediate family of her mistress. They were not seasonably informed of her suffering condition, or of her death.

Lastly, the author of this Memoir is a collateral descendant of Mrs. Wheatley, and has been familiar with the name and fame of Phillis from her childhood.

NOTE

Previous to Phillis's departure for Wilmington, she entrusted her papers to a daughter of the lady who received her on her return from that place. After her death, these papers were demanded by Peters, as the property of his deceased wife, and were, of course, yielded to his importunity. Some years after, he went to the South, and we have not been able to ascertain what eventually became of the manuscripts.

LETTER FROM
GEORGE WASHINGTON TO PHILLIS

We conclude with the following letter from George Washington to Phillis, which we find in Mr. Spark's edition of his life:—

CAMBRIDGE,
Feb. 28, 1776.,

MISS PHILLIS—

Your favor of the 26th of October did not reach my hands till the middle of December. Time enough, you will say, to have given an answer ere this. Granted. But a variety of important occurrences, continually interposing to distract the mind and withdraw the attention, I hope will apologize for the delay, and plead my excuse for the seeming but not real neglect. I thank you most sincerely for your polite notice of me in the elegant lines you enclosed: and however undeserving I may be of such encomium and panegyric, the style and manner exhibit a striking proof of your poetical talents; in honor of which, and as a tribute justly due to you, I would have published the poem had I not been apprehensive that, while I only meant to give the world this new instance of your genius, I might have incurred the imputation of vanity. This, and nothing else, determined me not to give it place in the public prints.

If you should ever come to Cambridge, or near headquarters, I shall be happy to see a person so favored by the Muses, and to whom nature has been so liberal and beneficent in her dispensations. I am, with great respect, your obedient, humble servant,

GEO. WASHINGTON.

POEMS

'Some view the sable race with scornful eye—
   Their color is a diabolic dye;
But know, ye Christians, Negroes black as Cain,
   May be refined, and join the angelic train.'

TO MÆCENAS

Mæcenas, you, beneath the myrtle shade,
Read o'er what poets sung, and shepherds played
What felt those poets, but you feel the same?
Does not your soul possess the sacred flame?
Their noble strains your equal genius shares
In softer language, and diviner airs.

While Homer paints, lo! circumfused in air,
Celestial Gods in mortal forms appear;
Swift as they move, hear each recess rebound;
Heaven quakes, earth trembles, and the shores resound.
Great Sire of verse, before my mortal eyes
The lightnings blaze across the vaulted skies;
And as the thunder shakes the heavenly plains,
A deep-felt horror thrills through all my veins.
When gentler strains demand thy graceful song,
The lengthening line moves languishing along,
When great Patroclus courts Achilles' aid,
The grateful tribute of my tears is paid:
Prone on the shore, he feels the pangs of love,
And stern Pelides' tenderest passions move.

Great Maro's strain in heavenly numbers flows,
The Nine inspire, and all the bosom glows.
Oh! could I rival thine and Virgil's page,
Or claim the Muses with the Mantuan sage;
Soon the same beauties should my mind adorn,
And the same ardors in my soul should burn:
Then should my song in bolder notes arise,

And all my numbers pleasingly surprise:
But here I sit and mourn, a grovelling mind
That fain would mount and ride upon the wind.

   Not you, my friend, these plaintive strains become;
Not you, whose bosom is the Muses' home.
When they from towering Helicon retire,
They fan in you the bright, immortal fire;
But I, less happy, cannot raise the song;
The faltering music dies upon my tongue.

   The happier Terence[5] all the choir inspired,
His soul replenished, and his bosom fired:
But say, ye Muses, why this partial grace
To one alone of Afric's sable race;
From age to age transmitting thus his name,
With the first glory in the realms of fame?

   Thy virtues, great Maecenas! shall be sung
In praise of him from whom those virtues sprung;
While blooming wreaths around thy temples spread,
I'll snatch a laurel from thine honored head,
While you, indulgent, smile upon the deed.

   As long as Thames in streams majestic flows,
Or Naiads in their oozy beds repose;
While Phoebus reigns above the starry train;
While bright Aurora purples o'er the main;
So long, great Sir, the Muse thy praise shall sing;
So long thy praise shall make Parnassus ring.
Then grant, Maecenas, thy paternal rays;
Hear me propitious, and defend my lays.

---

5   He was an African by birth.

ON VIRTUE

O thou bright jewel, in my aim I strive
To comprehend thee. Thine own words declare
Wisdom is higher than a fool can reach.
I cease to wonder and no more attempt
Thine height to explore, or fathom thy profound.
But O my soul, sink not into despair;
Virtue is near thee, and with gentle hand
Would now embrace thee,—hovers o'er thine head.
Fain would the heaven-born soul with her converse,
Then seek, then court her for her promised bliss.
Auspicious queen! thine heavenly pinions spread,
And lead celestial Chastity along.
Lo! now her sacred retinue descends,
Arrayed in glory from the orbs above.
Attend me, Virtue, through my youthful years;
Oh, leave me not to the false joys of time,
But guide my steps to endless life and bliss.
Greatness, or Goodness, say what shall I call thee,
To give an higher appellation still:
Teach me a better strain, a nobler lay,
O thou, enthroned with cherubs in the realms of day!

ON BRING BROUGHT
FROM AFRICA TO AMERICA

'T was mercy brought me from my pagan land,
Taught my benighted soul to understand
That there's a God — that there's a Saviour too;
Once I redemption neither sought nor knew.
Some view our sable race with scornful eye—
'Their color is a diabolic dye.'
Remember, Christians, Negroes black as Cain
May be refined, and join the angelic train.

TO THE UNIVERSITY
OF CAMBRIDGE,
IN NEW-ENGLAND

———————

While an intrinsic ardor prompts to write,
The Muses promise to assist my pen.
'T was not long since I left my native shore,

The land of errors and Egyptian gloom:

Father of mercy! 't was thy gracious hand
Brought me in safety from those dark abodes.

Students, to you 't is given to scan the heights
Above, to traverse the etherial space,
And mark the systems of revolving worlds.
Still more, ye sons of science, ye receive
The blissful news by messengers from heaven,
How Jesus' blood for your redemption flows.
See him, with hands outstretched upon the cross!
Immense compassion in his bosom glows;
He hears revilers, nor resents their scorn.
What matchless mercy in the Son of God!
He deigned to die, that they might rise again,
And share with him, in the sublimest skies,
Life without death, and glory without end.

Improve your privileges while they stay,
Ye pupils; and each hour redeem, that bears
Or good or bad report of you to heaven.

Let sin, that baneful evil to the soul,
By you be shunned; nor once remit your guard:
Suppress the deadly serpent in its egg,
Ye blooming plants of human race divine,
As Ethiop tells you, 't is your greatest foe;
Its transient sweetness turns to endless pain,
And in immense perdition sinks the soul.

TO THE KING'S
MOST EXCELLENT MAJESTY

1768

Your subjects hope, dread Sire, the crown upon your
    brows may flourish long,
And that your arm may in your God be strong.
Oh, may your sceptre num'rous nations sway,
And all with love and readiness obey.

But how shall we the British king reward?
Rule thou in peace, our father and our lord!
'Midst the remembrance of thy favors past,
The meanest peasants most admire the last.[6]

May George, beloved by all the nations round,
Live with Heaven's choicest, constant blessings crowned.
Great God! direct and guard him from on high,
And from his head let every evil fly;
And may each clime with equal gladness see
A monarch's smile can set his subjects free.

---

6   The repeal of the Stamp Act

ON THE DEATH OF
THE REV. DR. SEWELL

1769

Ere yet the morn its lovely blushes spread,
See Sewell numbered with the happy dead.
Hail, holy man! arrived the immortal shore;
Though we shall hear thy warning voice no more,
Come, let us all behold, with wishful eyes,
The saint ascending to his native skies:
From hence the prophet winged his rapturous way,
To the blest mansions in eternal day.
Then, begging for the Spirit of our God,
And panting eager for the same abode,
Come, let us all with the same vigor rise,
And take a prospect of the blissful skies;
While on our minds Christ's image is impressed,
And the dear Saviour glows in ev'ry breast.
Thrice happy saint! to find thy heaven at last,
What compensation for the evils past!
Great God! incomprehensible, unknown
By sense, we bow at thine exalted throne.
Oh, while we beg thine excellence to feel,
Thy sacred Spirit to our hearts reveal,
And give us of that mercy to partake,
Which thou hast promised for the Saviour's sake!

'Sewell is dead.' Swift-pinioned Fame thus cried.
'Is Sewell dead?' my trembling tongue replied.
Oh, what a blessing in his flight denied!
How oft for us the holy prophet prayed!
How oft to us the word of life conveyed!
By duty urged my mournful verse to close,
I for his tomb this epitaph compose.

"Lo, here, a man, redeemed by Jesus' blood,
"A sinner once, but now a saint with God.
"Behold, ye rich, ye poor, ye fools, ye wise,
"Nor let his monument your heart surprise;
" 'T will tell you what this holy man has done,
"Which gives him brighter lustre than the sun.
"Listen, ye happy, from your seats above;
"I speak sincerely, while I speak and love.
"He sought the paths of piety and truth,
"By these made happy from his early youth.
"In blooming years that grace divine he felt,
"Which rescues sinners from the chains of guilt.
"Mourn him, ye indigent, whom he has fed,
"And henceforth seek, like him, for living bread;
"Ev'n Christ, the bread descending from above,
"And ask an int'rest in his saving love.
"Mourn him, ye youth, to whom he oft has told
"God's gracious wonders, from the times of old.
"I, too, have cause, this mighty loss to mourn,
"For he, my monitor, will not return.
"Oh, when shall we to his blest state arrive?
"When the same graces in our bosoms thrive?"

ON THE DEATH OF THE
REV. MR. GEORGE WHITEFIELD

1770

Hail, happy saint! on thine immortal throne,
Possest of glory, life, and bliss unknown:
We hear no more the music of thy tongue;
Thy wonted auditories cease to throng.
Thy sermons in unequalled accents flowed,
And ev'ry bosom with devotion glowed;
Thou didst, in strains of eloquence refined,
Inflame the heart, and captivate the mind.
Unhappy, we the setting sun deplore,
So glorious once, but ah! it shines no more.

Behold the prophet in his towering flight!
He leaves the earth for heaven's unmeasured height,
And worlds unknown receive him from our sight.
There Whitefield wings with rapid course his way,
And sails to Zion through vast seas of day.
Thy prayers great saint, and thine incessant cries,
Have pierced the bosom of thy native skies.
Thou, moon, hast seen, and all the stars of light,
How he has wrestled with his God by night.
He prayed that grace in ev'ry heart might dwell;
He longed to see America excel;
He charged its youth that ev'ry grace divine
Should with full lustre in their conduct shine.
That Saviour, which his soul did first receive,

The greatest gift that ev'n a God can give,
He freely offered to the numerous throng,
That on his lips with list'ning pleasure hung.
   "Take him, ye wretched for your only good,
"Take him, ye starving sinners, for your food;
"Ye thirsty, come to this life-giving stream,
"Ye preachers, take him for your joyful theme;
"Take him, my dear Americans, he said,
"Be your complaints on his kind bosom laid:
"Take him, ye Africans, he longs for you;
"Impartial Saviour is his title due:
"Washed in the fountain of redeeming blood,
"You shall be sons, and kings, and priests to God."

   Great Countess,[7] we Americans revere
Thy name, and mingle in thy grief sincere;
New-England deeply feels, the orphans mourn,
Their more than father will no more return.
But though arrested by the hand of death,
Whitefield no more exerts his lab'ring breath,
Yet let us view him in the eternal skies,
Let ev'ry heart to this bright vision rise;
While the tomb, safe, retains its sacred trust,
Till life divine reanimates his dust.

---

7   The Countess of Huntingdon, to whom Mr. Whitefield
      was chaplain.

ON THE DEATH
OF A YOUNG LADY OF
FIVE YEARS OF AGE

From dark abodes to fair etherial light,
The enraptured innocent has winged her flight;
On the kind bosom of eternal love
She finds unknown beatitude above.
This know, ye parents, nor her loss deplore,
She feels the iron hand of pain no more;
The dispensations of unerring grace
Should turn your sorrows into grateful praise;
Let then no tears for her henceforward flow,
No more distressed in our dark vale below.
Her morning sun, which rose divinely bright,
Was quickly mantled with the gloom of night;
But hear in heaven's blest bowers your Nancy fair,
And learn to imitate her language there.

"Thou, Lord, whom I behold with glory crowned,
"By what sweet name, and in what tuneful sound
"Wilt thou be praised? Seraphic: powers are faint,
"Infinite love and majesty to paint.
"To thee let all their grateful voices raise,
"And saints and angels join their songs of praise."

Perfect in bliss, she, from her heavenly home,
Looks down, and smiling, beckons you to come.
Why then, fond parents, why those fruitless groans?
Restrain your tears, and cease your plaintive moans.

Freed from a world of sin, and snares, and pain,
Why would you wish your daughter back again?
No—bow resigned; let hope your grief control,
And check the rising tumult of the soul.
Calm in the prosperous and adverse day,
Adore tho God who gives and takes away;
Eye him in all, his holy name revere;
Upright your actions, and your hearts sincere;
Till, having sailed through life s tempestuous sea,
And from its rocks, and boisterous billows free,
Yourselves safe landed on the blissful shore,
Shall join your happy babe to part no more.

ON THE DEATH
OF A YOUNG GENTLEMAN

Who taught thee conflict with the powers of night,
To vanquish Satan in the fields of fight?
Who strung thy feeble arms with might unknown?
How great thy conquest, and how bright thy crown!
War with each princedom, throne, and power is o'er,
The scene is ended to return no more.
Oh, could my Muse thy seat on high behold,
How decked with laurel, how enriched with gold!
Oh, could she hear what praise thine harp employs,
How sweet thine anthems, how divine thy joys!
What heavenly grandeur should exalt her strain!
What holy raptures in her numbers reign!
To sooth the troubles of the mind to peace,
To still the tumult of life's tossing seas,
To ease the anguish of the parent's heart,
What shall my sympathizing verse impart?
Where is the balm to heal so deep a wound?
Where shall a sovereign remedy be found?
Look, gracious Spirit! from thy heavenly bower,
And thy full joys into their bosoms pour;
The raging tempest of their grief control,
And spread the dawn of glory through the soul,
To eye the path the saint departed trod,
And trace him to the bosom of his God.

TO A LADY ON
HER HUSBAND'S DEATH

Grim monarch! see, deprived of vital breath,
A young physician in the dust of death:
Dost thou go on incessant to destroy,
Our griefs to double and lay waste our joy?
Enough, thou never yet wast known to say,
Though millions die the vassals of thy sway:
Nor youth, nor science, nor the ties of love,
Nor aught on earth thy flinty heart can move.
The friend, the spouse, from his dire dart to save,
In vain we ask the sovereign of the grave.
Fair mourner, there see thy loved Leonard laid,
And o'er him spread the deep, impervious shade.
Closed are his eyes, and heavy fetters keep
His senses bound in never-waking sleep,
Till time shall cease, till many a starry world
Shall fall from heaven, in dire confusion hurled;
Till nature in her final wreck shall lie,
And her last groan shall rend the azure sky;
Not, not till then, his active soul shall claim
His body, a divine, immortal frame.

But see the softly-stealing tears apace
Pursue each other down the mourner's face:
But cease thy tears, bid every sigh depart,
And cast the load of anguish from thine heart:
From the cold shell of his great soul arise,
And look beyond, thou native of the skies;

There fix thy view, where, fleeter than the wind.
Thy Leonard mounts, and leaves the earth behind.
Thyself prepare to pass the vale of night,
To join forever on the hills of light.
To thine embrace his joyful spirit moves,
To thee, the partner of his earthly loves;
He welcomes thee to pleasures more refined,
And better suited to the immortal mind.

GOLIATH OF GATH

---

1 SAM. CHAP. 17ᵀᴴ

Ye martial powers, and all ye tuneful Nine,
Inspire my song, and aid my high design.
The dreadful scenes and toils of war I write,
The ardent warriors and the fields of fight:
You best remember, and you best can sing
The acts of heroes to the vocal string:
Resume the lays with which your sacred lyre
Did then the poet and the sage inspire.

Now front to front the armies were displayed,
Here Israel ranged, and there the foes arrayed;
The hosts on two opposing mountains stood,
Thick as the foliage of the waving wood.
Between them an extensive valley lay,
O'er which the gleaming armor poured the day;
When, from the camp of the Philistine foes,
Dreadful to view, a mighty warrior rose;
In the dire deeds of bleeding battle skilled,
The monster stalks, the terror of the field.
From Gath he sprung, Goliath was his name,
Of fierce deportment and gigantic frame:
A brazen helmet on his head was placed,
A coat of mail his form terrific graced;
The greaves his legs, the targe his shoulders prest;
Dreadful in arms, high towering o'er the rest,
A spear he proudly waved, whose iron head.

Strange to relate, six hundred shekels weighed:
He strode along, and shook the ample field,
While Phoebus blazed refulgent on his shield.
Through Jacob's race a chilling honor ran,
When thus the huge, enormous chief began:

  "Say, what the cause, that in this proud array,
"You set your battle in the face of day?
"One hero find in all your vaunting train,
"Then see who loses, and who wins the plain;
"For he who wins, in triumph may demand
"Perpetual service from the vanquished land:
"Your armies I defy, your force despise,
"By far inferior in Philistia's eyes:
"Produce a man and let us try the fight,
"Decide the contest, and the victor's right."
  Thus challenged he: all Israel stood amazed,
And ev'ry chief in consternation gazed;
But Jesse's son, in youthful bloom appears,
And warlike courage far beyond his years:
He left the folds, he left the flow'ry meads
And soft recesses of the sylvan shades.
Now Israel's monarch and his troops arise,
With peals of shouts ascending to the skies;
In Elab's vale, the scene of combat lies.

  When the fair morning blushed with orient red,
What David's sire enjoined, the son obeyed;
And swift of foot towards the trench he came,
Where glowed each bosom with the martial flame.
He leaves his carriage to another's care,
And runs to greet his brethren of the war.
While yet they spake the giant chief arose,
Repeats the challenge, and insults his foes.
Struck with the sound, and trembling at the view,
Affrighted Israel from its post withdrew.

"Observe ye this tremendous foe, they cry'd,
"Who in proud vaunts our armies hath defy'd?
"Whoever lays him prostrate on the plain,
"Freedom in Israel for his house shall gain;
"And on him wealth unknown the king will pour,
"And give his royal daughter for his dower."

Then Jesse's youngest hope:—"My brethren, say,
"What shall be done for him who takes away
"Reproach from Jacob, who destroys the chief,
"And puts a period to his country's grief?
"He vaunts the honors of his arms abroad,
"And scorns the armies of the living God."

Thus spoke the youth; the attentive people eyed
The wondrous hero, and again reply'd:
"Such the rewards our monarch will bestow
"On him who conquers and destroys his foe."
    Eliab heard, and kindled into ire,
To hear his shepherd brother thus inquire,
And thus begun: What errand brought thee, say,
"Who keeps thy flock? or does it go astray?
"I know the base ambition of thine heart,
"But back in safety from the field depart."

Eliab thus, to Jesse's youngest heir,
Expressed his wrath in accents most severe.
When to his brother mildly he replied,
"What have I done? or what the cause to chide?"

The words were told before the king, who sent
For the young hero to his royal tent.
Before the monarch, dauntless, he began;
"For this Philistine, fail no heart of man:
"I'll take the vale, and with the giant fight;

"I dread not all his boasts nor all his might."
When thus the king: "Durst thou, a stripling, go,
"And venture combat with so great a foe,
"Who all his days has been inured to fight,
"And made its deeds his study and delight?
"Battles and bloodshed brought the monster forth,
"And clouds and whirlwinds ushered in his birth."

  When David thus: " Ikept the fleecy care,
"And out there rushed a lion and a bear:
"A tender lamb the hungry lion took,
"And with no other weapon than my crook,
"Bold I pursued, and chased him o'er the field,
"The prey delivered, and the lion killed.
"As thus the lion and the bear I slew,
"So shall Goliath fall, and all his crew.
"The God who saved me from these beasts of prey,
"By me this monster in the dust shall lay."

  So David spoke. The wondering king reply'd;
"Go thou, with heaven and victory on thy side:
"This coat of mail, this sword, gird on," he said,
And placed a mighty helmet on his head.
The coat, the sword, the helm, he laid aside,
Nor chose to venture with those arms untry'd;
Then took his staff, and to the neighboring brook
Instant he ran, and thence five pebbles took.
Meantime descended to Philistia's son
A radiant cherub, and he thus begun:

"Goliath, well thou know'st thou hast defy'd
"Yon Hebrew armies, and their God deny'd.
"Rebellious wretch! audacious worm! forbear,
"Nor tempt the vengeance of their God too far:
"Those who with his omnipotence contend,

"No eye shall pity and no arm defend.
"Proud as thou art, in short-lived glory great,
"I come to tell thee thine approaching fate.
"Regard my words. The Judge of all the gods,
"Beneath whose steps the tow'ring mountain nods,
"Will give thine armies to the savage brood,
"That cut the liquid air, or range the wood.
"Thee, too, a well aimed pebble shall destroy,
"And thou shalt perish by a beardless boy.
"Such is the mandate from the realms above,
"And, should I try the vengeance to remove,
"Myself a rebel to my king would prove
"Goliath, say, shall grace to him be shown,
"Who dares heaven's monarch and insults his throne?"

"Your words are lost on me," the giant cries,
While fear and wrath contended in his eyes;
When thus the messenger from heaven replies:
"Provoke no more Jehovah's awful hand
"To hurl its vengeance on thy guilty land;
"He grasps the thunder, and he wings the storm,
"Servants, their sov'reign's orders to perform."

The angel spoke, and turned his eyes away,
Adding new radiance to the rising day.
Now David comes; the fatal stones demand
His left, the staff engaged his better hand.
The giant moved, and from his tow'ring height
Surveyed the stripling, and disdained the sight,
And thus began: "Am I a dog with thee?
"Bring'st thou no armor but a staff to me?
"The gods on thee their vollied curses pour,
"And beasts and birds of prey thy flesh devour."

David, undaunted, thus: "Thy spear and shield

"Shall no protection to thy body yield:
"Jehovah's name—no other arms I bear;
"I ask no other in this glorious war.
"To-day the Lord of Hosts to me will give
"Victory, to-day thy doom thou shalt receive;
"The fate you threaten shall your own become,
"And beasts shall be your animated tomb,
"That all the earth's inhabitants may know
"That there's a God who governs all below:
"This great assembly, too, shall witness stand,
"That needs not sword nor spear, the Almighty's hand:
"The battle his, the conquest he bestows,
"And to our power consigns our hated foes."

   Thus David spoke. Goliath heard, and came
To meet the hero in the field of fame.
Ah! fatal meeting to thy troops and thee;
But thou wast deaf to the divine decree:
Young David meets thee, meets thee not in vain;
'T is thine to perish on the ensanguined plain.

   And now the youth the forceful pebble flung;
Philistia trembled as it whizzed along.
In his dread forehead, where the helmet ends,
Just o'er the brows the well-aimed stone descends;
It pierced the skull, and shattered all the brain—
Prone on his face he tumbled to the plain.
Goliath's fall no smaller terror yields,
Than riving thunders in aerial fields:
The soul still lingered in its loved abode,
Till conquering David o'er the giant strode:
Goliath's sword then laid its roaster dead,
And from the body hewed the ghastly head;
The blood in gushing torrents drenched the plains,
The soul found passage through the spouting veins.

And now aloud the illustrious victor said,
"Where are your boastings, now your champion's dead?"
Scarce had he spoke, when the Philistines fled;
But fled in vain; the conqueror swift pursued:
What scenes of slaughter, and what pens of blood!
There, Saul, thy thousands grasped the empurpled sand
In pangs of death, the conquest of thine hand;
And David, there were thy ten thousands laid:
Thus Israel's damsels musically played.
   Near Gath and Ekron many a hero lay:
Breathed out their souls, and cursed the light of day:
Their fury, quenched by death, no longer burns,
And David with Goliath's head returns.
To Salem brought, but in his tent he placed
The load of armor which the giant graced.
His monarch saw him coming from the war,
And thus demanded of the son of Ner.
"Say, who is this amazing youth? " he cry'd,
When thus the leader of the host replied:
"As lives thy soul, I know not whence he sprung,
"So great in prowess, though in years so young."
"Inquire whose son is he," the sov'reign said,
"Before whose conquering arm Philistia fled."
Before the king behold tho stripling stand,
Goliath's head depending from his hand.
To him the king: "Say, of what martial line
"Art thou, young hero, and what sire was thine?"
He humbly thus: "The son of Jesse, I;
"I came the glories of the field to try.
"Small is my tribe, but valiant in the fight;
"Small is my city, but thy royal right"
"Then take the promised gifts," the monarch cry'd,
Conferring riches and the royal bride.
"Knit to my soul, forever thou remain
"With me, nor quit my regal roof again.

THOUGHTS ON THE
WORKS OF PROVIDENCE

———————————

Arise, my soul; on wings enraptured, rise,
To praise the Monarch of the earth and skies,
Whose goodness and beneficence appear,
As round its centre moves the rolling year;
Or when the morning glows with rosy charms,
Or the sun slumbers in the ocean's arms:
Of light divine be a rich portion lent,
To guide my soul and favor my intent.
Celestial Muse, my arduous flight sustain,
And raise my mind to a seraphic strain!

Adored forever be the God unseen,
Which round the sun revolves this vast machine,
Though to his eye its mass a point appears:
Adored the God that whirls surrounding spheres.
Which first ordained that mighty Sol should reign,
The peerless monarch of the etherial train:
Of miles twice forty millions is his height,
And yet his radiance dazzles mortal sight.
So far beneath—from him the extended earth
Vigor derives, and ev'ry flow'ry birth:
Vast through her orb she moves with easy grace,
Around her Phoebus in unbounded space;
True to her course, the impetuous storm derides,
Triumphant o'er the winds and surging tides.

Almighty, in these wondrous works of thine,
What Power, what Wisdom, and what Goodness shine!
And are thy wonders, Lord, by men explored,
And yet creating glory unadored?
Creation smiles in various beauty gay.
While day to night, and night succeeds to day:
That Wisdom which attends Jehovah's ways,
Shines most conspicuous in the solar rays:
Without them, destitute of heat and light,
This world would be the reign of endless night.
In their excess how would our race complain,
Abhorring life! how hate its lengthened chain!
From air, or dust, what numerous ills would rise!
What dire contagion taint the burning skies!
What pestilential vapor, fraught with death,
Would rise, and overspread the lands beneath!

Hail, smiling morn, that, from the orient main
Ascending, dost adorn the heavenly plain!
So rich, so various are thy beauteous dyes
That spread through all the circuit of the skies,
That, full of thee, my soul in rapture soars,
And thy great God, the cause of all, adores.
O'er beings infinite his love extends,
His Wisdom rules them, and his power defends.
When tasks diurnal tire the human frame,
The spirits faint, and dim the vital flame;
Then, too, that ever-active bounty shines,
Which not infinity of space confines.
The sable veil, that Night in silence draws,
Conceals effects, but shews the Almighty Cause;
Night seals in sleep the wide creation fair,
And all is peaceful but the brow of care.
Again, gay Phœbus, as the day before,
Wakes ev'ry eye, but what shall wake no more;

Again the face of nature is renewed,
Which still appears harmonious, fair, and good.
May grateful strains salute the smiling morn,
Before its beams the eastern hills adorn!

   Shall day to day and night to night conspire
To show the goodness of the Almighty Sire?
This mental voice shall man regardless hear,
And never, never raise the filial prayer?
To-day, oh hearken, nor your folly mourn
For time misspent, that never will return.

   But see the sons of vegetation rise,
And spread their leafy banners to the skies.
All-wise, Almighty Providence, we trace
In trees and plants, and all the flow'ry race,
As clear as in the noble frame of man,
All lovely copies of the Maker's plan,—
The power the same that forms a ray of light,
That called creation from eternal night.
"Let there be light," he said: from his profound
Old Chaos heard, and trembled at the sound:
Swift as the word, inspired by power divine,
Behold the light around its Maker shine,
The first fair product of the omnific God,
And now through all his works diffused abroad.

   As reason's powers by day our God disclose,
So we may trace him in the night's repose:
Say, what is sleep? and dreams how passing strange!
When action ceases and ideas range
Licentious and unbounded o'er the plains,
Where fancy's queen in giddy triumph reigns.
Hear in soft strains the dreaming lover sigh
To a kind fair, or rave in jealousy;

On pleasure now, and now on vengeance bent,
The lab'ring passions struggle for a vent.
What power, O man! thy reason then restores,
So long suspended in nocturnal hours?
What secret hand returns the mental train,
And gives improved thine active powers again?
From thee, O man, what gratitude should rise!
And when from balmy sleep thou op'st thine eyes,
Let thy first thoughts be praises to the skies.
How merciful our God, who thus imparts
O'erflowing tides of joy to human hearts,
When wants and woes might be our righteous lot,
Our God forgetting, by our God forgot!

    Among the mental powers a question rose,
What most the image of the Eternal shows;
When thus to reason (so let Fancy rove,)
Her great companion spoke, immortal Love:

"Say, mighty power, how long shall strife prevail,
"And with its murmurs load the whispering gale?
"Refer the cause to Recollection's shrine,
"Who loud proclaims my origin divine,
"The cause whence heaven and earth began to be,
"And is not man immortalized by me?
"Reason, let this most causeless strife subside."
Thus love pronounced, and reason thus reply'd:
    "Thy birth, celestial queen! 't is mine to own,
"In thee resplendent is the Godhead shown;
"Thy words persuade, my soul enraptured feels
"Resistless beauty which thy soul reveals."
Ardent she spoke, and kindling at her charms,
She clasped the blooming goddess in her arms.

Infinite Love, where'er we turn our eyes,
Appears: this ev'ry creature's want supplies;
This most is heard in Nature's constant voice;
This makes the morn, and this the eve, rejoice;
This bids the fostering rains and dews descend,
To nourish all, to serve one gen'ral end,
The good of man: yet man ungrateful pays
But little homage, and but little praise.
To him whose works arrayed in mercy shine,
What songs should rise, how constant, how divine!

TO A LADY, ON THE
DEATH OF THREE RELATIONS

—————————————

We trace the power of death from tomb to tomb,
And his are all the ages yet to come.
'T is his to call the planets from on high,
To blacken Phœbus, and dissolve the sky;
His too, when all in his dark realms are hurled,
From its firm base to shake the solid world;
His fatal sceptre rules the spacious whole,
And trembling nature rocks from pole to pole.
　Awful he moves, and wide his wings are spread:
Behold thy brother numbered with the dead:
From bondage freed, the exulting spirit flies
Beyond Olympus, and these starry skies.
Lost in our woe for thee, blest shade, we mourn
In vain; to earth thou never must return.
Thy sisters, too , fair mourner, feel the dart
Of death, and with fresh torture rend thine heart.
Weep not for them, who wish thine happy mind
To rise with them and leave the world behind.

　As a young plant by hurricanes upturn,
So near its parent lies the newly born—
But midst the bright etherial train, behold,
It shines superior on a throne of gold;
Then mourner, cease; let hope thy tears restrain,
Smile on the tomb, and soothe the raging pain,
On yon blest regions fix thy longing view,
Mindless of sublunary scenes below;

Ascend the sacred mount, in thought arise,
And seek substantial and immortal joys;
Where hope receives, where faith to vision springs,
And raptured seraphs tune the immortal strings
To strains extatic. Thou the chorus join,
And to thy father tune the praise divine.

THOUGHTS ON
THE WORKS OF PROVIDENCE

Arise, my soul; on wings enraptured, rise,
To praise the Monarch of the earth and skies,
Whose goodness and beneficence appear,
As round its centre moves the rolling year;
Or when the morning glows with rosy charms,
Or the sun slumbers in the ocean's arms:
Of light divine be a rich portion lent,
To guide my soul and favor my intent.
Celestial Muse, my arduous flight sustain,
And raise my mind to a seraphic strain!

Adored forever be the God unseen,
Which round the sun revolves this vast machine,
Though to his eye its mass a point appears:
Adored the God that whirls surrounding spheres.
Which first ordained that mighty Sol should reign,
The peerless monarch of the etherial train:
Of miles twice forty millions is his height,
And yet his radiance dazzles mortal sight.
So far beneath—from him the extended earth
Vigor derives, and ev'ry flow'ry birth:
Vast through her orb she moves with easy grace,
Around her Phoebus in unbounded space;
True to her course, the impetuous storm derides,
Triumphant o'er the winds and surging tides.

Almighty, in these wondrous works of thine,
What Power, what Wisdom, and what Goodness shine!
And are thy wonders, Lord, by men explored,
And yet creating glory unadored?
Creation smiles in various beauty gay.
While day to night, and night succeeds to day:
That Wisdom which attends Jehovah's ways,
Shines most conspicuous in the solar rays:
Without them, destitute of heat and light,
This world would be the reign of endless night.
In their excess how would our race complain,
Abhorring life! how hate its lengthened chain!
From air, or dust, what numerous ills would rise!
What dire contagion taint the burning skies!
What pestilential vapor, fraught with death,
Would rise, and overspread the lands beneath!

Hail, smiling morn, that, from the orient main
Ascending, dost adorn the heavenly plain!
So rich, so various are thy beauteous dyes
That spread through all the circuit of the skies,
That, full of thee, my soul in rapture soars,
And thy great God, the cause of all, adores.
O'er beings infinite his love extends,
His Wisdom rules them, and his power defends.
When tasks diurnal tire the human frame,
The spirits faint, and dim the vital flame;
Then, too, that ever-active bounty shines,
Which not infinity of space confines.
The sable veil, that Night in silence draws,
Conceals effects, but shews the Almighty Cause;
Night seals in sleep the wide creation fair,
And all is peaceful but the brow of care.
Again, gay Phœbus, as the day before,
Wakes ev'ry eye, but what shall wake no more;

HYMN TO THE MORNING

Attend my lays, ye ever honored Nine,
Assist my labors, and my strains refine;
In smoothest numbers pour the notes along.
For bright Aurora now demands my song.

Aurora hail! and all the thousand dies
Which deck thy progress through the vaulted skies
The morn awakes, and wide extends her rays,
On ev'ry leaf the gentle zephyr plays;
Harmonious lays the feathered race resume,
Dart the bright eye, and shake the painted plume.

Ye shady groves, your verdant bloom display,
To shield your poet from the burning day:
Calliope, awake the sacred lyre,
While thy fair sisters fan the pleasing fire.
The bowers, the gales, the variegated skies,
In all their pleasures in my bosom rise.

See in the east, the illustrious king of day!
His rising radiance drives the shades away—
But oh! I feel his fervid beams too strong,
And scarce begun, concludes the abortive song.

HYMN TO THE EVENING

Soon as the sun forsook the eastern main,
The pealing thunder shook the heavenly plain;
Majestic grandeur! From the zephyr's wing,
Exhales the incense of the blooming spring.
Soft purl the streams, the birds renew their notes,
And through the air their mingled music floats.

Through all the heavens what beauteous dyes are spread,
But the west glories in the deepest red:
So may our breasts with ev'ry virtue glow,
The living temples of our God below!

Filled with the praise of him who gives the light,
And draws the sable curtains of the night,
Let placid slumbers soothe each weary mind,
At morn to wake, more heavenly, more refined;
So shall the labors of the day begin
More pure, more guarded from the snares of sin.
Night's leaden sceptre seals my drowsy eyes,
Then cease my song, till fair Aurora rise.

ISAIAH,
63D CHAP. 1ST AND 8TH VERSES

Say, heavenly Muse, what king, or mighty God,
That moves sublime from Idumea's road?
In Bozrah's dyes, with martial glories joined,
His purple vesture waves upon the wind.
Why thus enrobed delights he to appear
In the dread image of the Power of war?
Compressed in wrath, the swelling wine-press groaned;
It bled, and poured the gushing purple round.

"Mine was the art," the Almighty Saviour said,
And shook the dazzling glories of his head;
"When all forsook, I trod the press alone,
"And conquered by omnipotence my own;
"For man's release sustained the ponderous load,
"For man the wrath of an immortal God;
"To execute the Eternal's dread command,
"My soul I sacrificed with willing hand;
"Sinless I stood before the avenging frown,
"Atoning thus, for vices not my own."

His eye the ample field of battle round
Surveyed, but no created succors found;
His own omnipotence sustained the fight,
His vengeance sunk the haughty foes in night,
Beneath his feet the prostrate troops were spread,
And round him lay the dying and the dead.

Great God, what lightning flashes from thine eyes!
What power withstands if thou indignant rise?

Against thy Zion though her foes may rage,
And all their cunning, all their strength engage,
Yet she serenely on thy bosom lies,
Smiles at their arts, and all their force defies.

ON RECOLLECTION

Mneme begin Inspire, ye sacred Nine,
Your vent'rous Afric, in her great design.
Mneme, immortal power, I trace thy spring;
Assist my strains, while I thy glories sing:
The acts of long departed yours by thee
Recovered, in due order ranged we see:
Thy power the long-forgotten calls from night,
That sweetly plays before the fancy's sight.

Mneme in our nocturnal visions pours
The ample treasure of her secret stores;
Swift from above, she wings her silent flight
Through Phebe's realms, fair regent of the night,
And, in her pomp of images displayed,
To the high-raptured poet gives her aid;
Through the unbounded regions of the mind,
Diffusing light, celestial and refined.
The heavenly phantom paints the actions done
By every tribe beneath the rolling sun.

Mneme, enthroned within the human breast,
Has vice condemned, and every virtue blest.
How sweet the sound when we her plaudit hear!
Sweeter than music to the ravished ear,
Sweeter than Maro's entertaining strains,
Resounding through the groves, and hills, and plains.
But how is Mneme dreaded by the race
Who scorn her warnings, and despise her grace!
By her unveiled each horrid crime appears,

Her awful hand a cup of wormwood bears.
Days, years, misspent, oh what a hell of woe!
Hers the worst tortures that the soul can know.

Now eighteen years their destined course have run.
In fast succession round the central sun.
How did the follies of that period pass
Unnoticed, but behold them writ in brass!
In Recollection see them fresh return,
And sure 'tis mine to be ashamed and mourn.

O Virtue! smiling in immortal green,
Do thou exert thy power, and change the scene;
Be thine employ to guide my future days,
And mine to pay the tribute of my praise.

Of Recollection such the power enthroned
In every breast, and thus her power is owned.
The wretch who dared the vengeance of the skies,
At last awakes in horror and surprise,
By her alarmed, he sees impending fate,
But howls in anguish and repents too late.

But oh! what peace, what joys are hers to impart
To ev'ry holy, ev'ry upright heart!
Thrice blest the man, who, in her sacred shrine,
Feels himself sheltered from the wrath divine!

ON IMAGINATION

Thy various works, imperial queen, we see
How bright their forms! how decked with pomp by thee!
Thy wond'rous acts in beauteous order stand,
And all attest how potent is thine hand.
　From Helicon's refulgent heights attend,
Ye sacred choir, and my attempts befriend:
To tell her glories with a faithful tongue,
Ye blooming graces, triumph in my song.
Now here, now there, the roving Fancy flies,
Till some loved object strikes her wand'ring eyes,
Whose silken fetters all the senses bind,
And soft captivity involves the mind.

　Imagination! who can sing thy force?
Or who describe the swiftness of thy course?
Soaring through air to find the bright abode,
The empyreal palace of the thundering God,
We on thy pinions can surpass the wind,
And leave the rolling universe behind:
From star to star the mental optics rove,
Measure the skies, and range the realms above.
There in one view we grasp the mighty whole,
Or with new worlds amaze the unbounded soul.

　Though Winter frowns, to Fancy's raptured eyes
The fields may flourish, and gay scenes arise;
The frozen deeps may burst their iron bands,
And bid their waters murmur o'er the sands.
Fair Flora may resume her fragrant reign,

And with her flowery riches deck the plain;
Sylvanus may diffuse his honors round,
And all the forests may with leaves be crowned;
Showers may descend, and dews their gems disclose,
And nectar sparkle on the blooming rose.

Such is thy power, nor are thine orders vain.
O thou, the leader of the mental train:
In full perfection all thy works are wrought,
And thine the sceptre o'er the realms of thought;
Before thy throne the subject passions bow,
Of subject-passions sov'reign ruler Thou;
At thy command joy rushes on the heart,
And through the glowing veins the spirits dart.

Fancy might now her silken pinions try
To rise from earth, and sweep the expanse on high;
From Tithon's bed now might Aurora rise,
Her cheeks all glowing with celestial dyes,
While a pure stream of light o'erflows the skies.
The monarch of the day I might behold,
And all the mountains tipt with radiant gold,
But I reluctant leave the pleasing views,
Which Fancy dresses to delight the Muse;
Winter austere forbids me to aspire,
And northern tempests damp the rising fire;
They chill the tides of Fancy's flowing sea,—
Cease then my song, cease then the unequal lay.

A FUNERAL POEM

ON THE DEATH OF C***** E*****,
AN INFANT OF TWELVE MONTHS

 Through airy roads he wings his instant flight
To purer regions of celestial light;
Enlarged he sees unnumbered systems roll,
Beneath him sees the universal whole;
Planets on planets run their destined round,
And circling wonders fill the vast profound.
The etherial now, and now the empyreal skies
With growing splendors strike his wondering eyes:
The angels view him with delight unknown,
Press his soft hand, and seat him on the throne;
Then, smiling, thus: "To this divine abode,
"The seat of saints, of seraphs, and of God,
"Thrice welcome thou." The raptured babe replies:
"Thanks to my God, who snatched me to the skies,
"Ere vice triumphant had possessed my heart,
"Ere yet the tempter had beguiled my heart,
"Ere yet on sin's base actions I was bent,
"Ere yet I knew temptation's dire intent,
"Ere yet the lash for horrid crimes I felt,
"Ere vanity had led the way to guilt;
"But soon arrived at my celestial goal,
"Full glories rush on my expanding soul."
Joyful he spoke: exulting cherubs round
Clapt their glad wings; the heavenly vaults resound.

Say, parents, why this unavailing moan?
Why heave your pensive bosoms with the groan?
To Charles, the happy subject of my song,
A brighter world, and nobler strains belong.
Say, would you tear him from the realms above,
By thoughtless wishes and preposterous love?
Does his felicity increase your pain?
Or could you welcome to this world again
The heir of bliss? With a superior air
Methinks he answers with a smile severe,—
"Thrones and dominions cannot tempt me there."
But still you cry, "Can we the sigh forbear,
"And still, and still must we not pour the tear?
"Our only hope, more dear than vital breath,
"Twelve moons revolved, becomes the prey of death;
"Delightful infant, nightly visions give
"Thee to our arms, and we with joy receive;
"We fain would clasp the phantom to our breast,
"The phantom flies, and leaves the soul unblest."

To yon bright regions let your faith ascend;
Prepare to meet your dearest infant friend
In pleasures without measure, without end.

TO CAPTAIN H******D

OF THE 65TH REGIMENT

Say, Muse divine, can hostile scenes delight
The warrior's bosom in the fields of fight?
Lo! here the Christian and the hero join
With mutual grace to form the man divine.
In H———d see, with pleasure and surprise,
Where valor kindles, and where virtue lies:
Go, hero brave, still grace the post of fame,
And add new glories to thine honored name,
Still to the field, and still to virtue true:
Britannia glories in no son like you.

TO THE RIGHT
HONORABLE WILLIAM,
EARL OF DARTMOUTH

HIS MAJESTY'S PRINCIPAL SECRETARY
OF STATE FOR NORTH AMERICA, &C.

Hail, happy day! when, smiling like the morn,
Fair Freedom rose, New-England to adorn:
The northern clime, beneath her genial ray,
Dartmouth! congratulates thy blissful sway;
Elate with hope, her race no longer mourns,
Each soul expands, each grateful bosom burns,
While in thine hand with pleasure we behold
The silken reins, and Freedom's charms unfold.
Long lost to realms beneath the northern skies,
She shines supreme, while hated faction dies:
Soon as appeared the Goddess long desired,
Sick at the view she languished and expired;
Thus from the splendors of the morning light
The owl in sadness seeks the caves of night.

No more, America, in mournful strain,
Of wrongs and grievance unredressed complain;
No longer shall thou dread the iron chain
Which wanton Tyranny, with lawless hand,
Has made, and with it meant t'enslave the land.
Should you, my lord, while you peruse my song,
Wonder from whence my love of Freedom sprung,
Whence flow these wishes for the common good,

By feeling hearts alone best understood,
I, young in life, by seeming cruel fate
Was snatched from Afric's fancied happy seat:
What pangs excruciating must molest,
What sorrows labor in my parent's breast!
Steeled was that soul, and by no misery moved,
That from a father seized his babe beloved:
Such, such my case. And can I then but pray
Others may never feel tyrannic sway?

For favors past, great Sir, our thanks are due,
And thee we ask thy favors to renew,
Since in thy power, as in thy will before,
To soothe the griefs which thou didst once deplore.
May heavenly grace the sacred sanction give
To all thy works, and thou forever live,
Not only on the wings of fleeting Fame,
Though praise immortal crowns the patriot's name,
But to conduct to heaven's refulgent fane,
May fiery coursers sweep the etherial plain,
And bear thee upwards to that blest abode,
Where, like the prophet, thou shalt find thy God.

ODE TO NEPTUNE

ON MRS. W———'S VOYAGE TO ENGLAND

While raging tempests shake the shore,
While Æolas' thunders round us roar,
And sweep impetuous o'er the plain,
Be still, O tyrant of the main;
Nor let thy brow contracted frowns betray,
While my Susannah skims the watery way.

The Power propitious hears the lay,
The blue-eyed daughters of the sea
With sweeter cadence glide along,
And Thames responsive joins the song.
Pleased with their note, Sol sheds benign his ray,
And double radiance decks the face of day.

To court thee to Britannia's arms,
Serene the clime and mild the sky,
Her region boasts unnumbered charms;
Thy welcome smiles in ev'ry eye.
Thy promise, Neptune, keep; record my prayer,
Nor give my wishes to the empty air.

BOSTON,
October 10, 1772.

TO A LADY

ON HER COMING TO NORTH AMERICA WITH HER SON, FOR THE RECOVERY OF HER HEALTH

Indulgent Muse! my groveling mind inspire,
And fill my bosom with celestial fire.

See from Jamaica's fervid shores she moves,
Like the fair mother of the blooming loves,
When from above the Goddess, with her hand,
Fans the soft breeze, and lights upon the land;
Thus she, on Neptune's watery realm reclined,
Appeared, and thus invites the lingering wind.

"Arise, ye winds, America explore,
"Waft me, ye gales, from this malignant shore;
"The northern milder climes I long to greet,
"There, hope that health will my arrival meet."

Soon as she spoke, in my ideal view,
The winds assented, and the vessel flew.
Madam, your spouse, bereft of wife and son,
In the grove's dark recesses pours his moan;
Each branch, wide spreading to the ambient sky,
Forgets its verdure, and submits to die.

From thence I turn, and leave the sultry plain,
And swift pursue thy passage o'er the main:
The ship arrives before the fav'ring wind,
And makes the Philadelphian port assigned;
Thence I attend you to Bostonia's arms,
Where gen'rous friendship ev'ry bosom warms:
Thrice welcome here! may health revive again,
Bloom on thy cheek, and bound in ev'ry vein!
Then back return to gladden ev'ry heart,
And give your spouse his soul's far dearer part;
Received again, with what a sweet surprise,
The tear in transport starting from his eyes!
While his attendant son, with blooming grace,
Springs to his father's ever dear embrace,
With shouts of joy Jamaica s rocks resound,
With shouts of joy the country rings around.

TO A LADY

ON HER REMARKABLE PRESERVATION
IN A HURRICANE, IN NORTH CAROLINA

Though thou didst hear the tempest from afar,
And felt'st the horrors of the watery war,
To me unknown, yet on this peaceful shore
Methinks I hear the storm tumultuous roar,
And how stern Boreas, with impetuous hand,
Compelled the Nereids to usurp the land.
Reluctant rose the daughters of the main,
And slow ascending, glided o'er the plain,
Till Æolus in his rapid chariot drove,
In gloomy grandeur from the vaults above.
Furious he comes; his winged sons obey
Their frantic sire, and madden all the sea.
The billows rave, the wind's fierce tyrant roars,
And with his thundering terrors shakes the shores:
Broken by waves, the vessel's frame is rent,
And strews with planks the watery element.

But thee, Maria, a kind Nereid's shield
Preserved from sinking, and thy form upheld:
And sure some heavenly oracle designed,
At that dread crisis, to instruct thy mind
Things of eternal consequence to weigh,
And to thine heart just feelings to convey
Of things above, and of the future doom,
And what the births of the dread world to come.

From tossing seas I welcome thee to land.
"Resign her, Nereid," 'twas thy God's command.
Thy spouse, late buried, as thy fears conceived,
Again returns, thy fears are all relieved:
Thy daughter, blooming with celestial grace,
Again thou see'st, again thine arms embrace;
Oh come, and joyful show thy spouse his heir,
And what the blessings of maternal care!

TO A LADY AND
HER CHILDREN

ON THE DEATH OF
HER SON AND THEIR BROTHER

O'erwhelming sorrow now demands my song:
From death the overwhelming sorrow sprung.
What flowing tears! what hearts with grief opprest!
What sighs on sighs heave the fond parent's breast!
The brother weeps, the hapless sisters join
The increasing woe, and swell the crystal brine;
The poor, who once his generous bounty fed,
Droop and bewail their benefactor dead.
In death the friend, the kind companion lies,
And in one'death what various comfort dies!

The unhappy mother sees the sanguine rill
Forget to flow, and nature's wheels stand still:
But see, from earth his spirit far removed,
And know no grief recals your best beloved:
He, upon pinions swifter than the wind,
Has left mortality's sad scenes behind
For joys to this terrestrial state unknown,
And glories richer than the monarch's crown.
Of virtue's steady coarse the prize behold!
What blissful wonders to his mind unfold!
But of celestial joys I sing in vain:
Attempt not, Muse, the too adventurous strain.
No more in briny showers ye friends around.

Or bathe his clay, or waste them on the ground.
Still do you weep, still wish for his return?
How cruel thus to weep and thus to mourn!
No more for him the streams of sorrow pour
But haste to join him on the heavenly shore,
On harps of gold to tune immortal lays,
And to your God immortal anthems raise.

TO A
GENTLEMAN AND LADY

ON THE DEATH OF THE LADY'S
BROTHER AND SISTER, AND A CHILD OF
THE NAME OF AVIS, AGED ONE YEAR

On Death's domain intent I fix my eyes,
Where human nature in vast ruin lies:
With pensive mind I search the drear abode,
Where the dread conquerer has his spoils bestowed;
There, there the offspring of six thousand years,
In endless numbers to my view appears:
Whole kingdoms in his gloomy den are thrust,
And nations mix with their primeval dust;
Insatiate still, he gluts the ample tomb;
His is the present, his the age to come.
See here a brother, here a sister spread,
And a sweet daughter mingled with the dead.

But, Madam, let your grief be laid aside,
And let the fountain of your tears be dried.
In vain they flow to wet the dusty plain,
Your sighs are wafted to the skies in vain;
Your pains they witness, but they can no more,
While Death reigns tyrant o'er this mortal shore.

The glowing stars and silver queen of light
At last must perish in the gloom of night;
Resign thy friends to that Almighty hand

Which gave them life, and bow to his command;
Thine Avis give without a murmuring heart,
Though half thy soul be fated to depart.
To shining guards consign thine infant care,
To waft triumphant through the seas of air:
Her soul, enlarged, to heavenly pleasure springs,
She feeds on truth and uncreated things.
Methinks I hear her in the realms above,
And leaning forward with a filial love,
Invite you there to share immortal bliss
Unknown, untasted in a state like this.
With tow'ring hopes, and growing grace arise,
And seek beatitude beyond the skies.

ON THE DEATH OF
DR. SAMUEL MARSHALL

1771

Through thickest glooms look back, immortal shade,
On that confusion which thy death has made:
Or from Olympus' height look down, and see
A Town involv'd in grief bereft of thee.
Thy Lucy sees thee mingle with the dead,
And rends the graceful tresses from her head,
Wild in her woe, with grief unknown opprest
Sigh follows sigh deep heaving from her breast.

Too quickly fled, ah! whither art thou gone?
Ah! lost for ever to thy wife and son!
The hapless child, thine only hope and heir,
Clings round his mother's neck, and weeps his sorrows there.
The loss of thee on Tyler's soul returns,
And Boston for her dear physician mourns.

When sickness call'd for Marshall's healing hand,
With what compassion did his soul expand?
In him we found the father and the friend:
In life how lov'd! how honour'd in his end!
And must not then our AEsculapius stay
To bring his ling'ring infant into day?
The babe unborn in the dark womb is tost,
And seems in anguish for its father lost.

Gone is Apollo from his house of earth,
But leaves the sweet memorials of his worth:
The common parent, whom we all deplore,
From yonder world unseen must come no more,
Yet 'midst our woes immortal hopes attend
The spouse, the sire, the universal friend.

TO A GENTLEMAN

ON HIS VOYAGE TO GREAT BRITAIN
FOR THE RECOVERY OF HIS HEALTH

While others chant of gay Elysian scenes,
Of balmy zephyrs, and of flowery plains,
My song, more happy, speaks a greater name,
Feels higher motives and a nobler flame.
For thee, Oh R———, the Muse attunes her strings,
And mounts sublime above inferior things.

I sing not now of green embow'ring woods,
I sing not now the daughters of the floods,
I sing not of the storms o'er ocean driven,
And how they howled along the waste of heaven;
But I to R——— would paint the British shore,
And vast Atlantic not untry'd before:
Thy life impaired, commands thee to arise,
Leave these bleak regions and inclement skies,
Where chilling winds return the winter past,
And nature shudders at the furious blast.

O thou stupendous, earth-enclosing main,
Exert thy wonders to the world again!
If e'er thy power prolonged the fleeting breath,
Turned back the shafts, and mocked the gates of death,
If e'er thine air dispensed a healing power,
Or snatched the victim from the fatal hour,
This equal case demands thine equal care,

And equal wonders may this patient share.
But unavailing, frantic is the dream,
To hope thine aid without the aid of Him
Who gave thee birth, and taught thee where to flow,
And in thy waves his various blessings show.

May R——— return to view his native shore,
Replete with vigor not his own before;
Then shall we see with pleasure and surprise,
And own thy work, great Ruler of the skies!

TO THE
REV. DR. THOMAS AMORY

ON READING HIS SERMONS ON
DAILY DEVOTION, IN WHICH THAT DUTY
IS RECOMMENDED AND ASSISTED

To cultivate in ev'ry noble mind
Habitual grace, and sentiments refin'd,
Thus while you strive to mend the human heart,
Thus while the heav'nly precepts you impart,
O may each bosom catch the sacred fire,
And youthful minds to Virtue's throne aspire!

When God's eternal ways you set in sight,
And Virtue shines in all her native light,
In vain would Vice her works in night conceal,
For Wisdom's eye pervades the sable veil.

Artists may paint the sun's effulgent rays,
But Amory's pen the brighter God displays:
While his great works in Amory's pages shine,
And while he proves his essence all divine,
The Atheist sure no more can boast aloud
Of chance, or nature, and exclude the God;
As if the clay without the potter's aid
Should rise in various forms, and shapes self-made,
Or worlds above with orb o'er orb profound
Self-mov'd could run the everlasting round.

It cannot be—unerring Wisdom guides
With eye propitious, and o'er all presides.

   Still prosper, Amory! still may'st thou receive
The warmest blessings which a muse can give,
And when this transitory state is o'er,
When kingdoms fall, and fleeting Fame's no more,
May Amory triumph in immortal fame,
A nobler title, and superior name!

ON THE DEATH
OF J. C. AN INFANT

NO more the flow'ry scenes of pleasure rife,
Nor charming prospects greet the mental eyes,
No more with joy we view that lovely face
Smiling, disportive, flush'd with ev'ry grace.
    The tear of sorrow flows from ev'ry eye,
Groans answer groans, and sighs to sighs reply;
What sudden pangs shot thro' each aching heart,
When, Death, thy messenger dispatch'd his dart?
Thy dread attendants, all-destroying Pow'r,
Hurried the infant to his mortal hour.
Could'st thou unpitying close those radiant eyes?
Or fail'd his artless beauties to surprise?
Could not his innocence thy stroke controul,
Thy purpose shake, and soften all thy soul?
    The blooming babe, with shades of Death o'er-spread,
No more shall smile, no more shall raise its head,
But, like a branch that from the tree is torn,
Falls prostrate, wither'd, languid, and forlorn.
"Where flies my James?" 'tis thus I seem to hear
The parent ask, "Some angel tell me where
"He wings his passage thro' the yielding air?"
Methinks a cherub bending from the skies
Observes the question, and serene replies,
"In heav'ns high palaces your babe appears:
"Prepare to meet him, and dismiss your tears."
Shall not th' intelligence your grief restrain,
And turn the mournful to the cheerful strain?

Cease your complaints, suspend each rising sigh,
Cease to accuse the Ruler of the sky.
Parents, no more indulge the falling tear:
Let Faith to heav'n's refulgent domes repair,
There see your infant, like a seraph glow:
What charms celestial in his numbers flow
Melodious, while the foul-enchanting strain
Dwells on his tongue, and fills th' ethereal plain?
Enough—for ever cease your murm'ring breath;
Not as a foe, but friend converse with Death,
Since to the port of happiness unknown
He brought that treasure which you call your own.
The gift of heav'n intrusted to your hand
Cheerful resign at the divine command:
Not at your bar must sov'reign Wisdom stand.

AN HYMN
TO HUMANITY

TO S. P. G. ESQ;

I

LO! for this dark terrestrial ball
Forsakes his azure-paved hall
   A prince of heav'nly birth!
Divine Humanity behold,
What wonders rise, what charms unfold
   At his descent to earth!

II

The bosoms of the great and good
With wonder and delight he view'd,
   And fix'd his empire there:
Him, close compressing to his breast,
The sire of gods and men address'd,
   "My son, my heav'nly fair!

III

"Descend to earth, there place thy throne;
"To succour man's afflicted son
   "Each human heart inspire:
"To act in bounties unconfin'd
"Enlarge the close contracted mind,
   "And fill it with thy fire."

IV

Quick as the word, with swift career
He wings his course from star to star,
   And leaves the bright abode.
The Virtue did his charms impart;
Their G——-! then thy raptur'd heart
   Perceiv'd the rushing God:

V

For when thy pitying eye did see
The languid muse in low degree,
   Then, then at thy desire
Descended the celestial nine;
O'er me methought they deign'd to shine,
   And deign'd to string my lyre.

VI

Can Afric's muse forgetful prove?
Or can such friendship fail to move
   A tender human heart?
Immortal Friendship laurel-crown'd
The smiling Graces all surround
   With ev'ry heav'nly Art.

TO THE
HONOURABLE T. H. ESQ;

ON THE DEATH OF HIS DAUGHTER

WHILE deep you mourn beneath the cypress-shade
The hand of Death, and your dear daughter laid
In dust, whose absence gives your tears to flow,
And racks your bosom with incessant woe,
Let Recollection take a tender part,
Assuage the raging tortures of your heart,
Still the wild tempest of tumultuous grief,
And pour the heav'nly nectar of relief:
Suspend the sigh, dear Sir, and check the groan,
Divinely bright your daughter's Virtues shone:
How free from scornful pride her gentle mind,
Which ne'er its aid to indigence declin'd!
Expanding free, it sought the means to prove
Unfailing charity, unbounded love!

She unreluctant flies to see no more
Her dear-lov'd parents on earth's dusky shore:
Impatient heav'n's resplendent goal to gain,
She with swift progress cuts the azure plain,
Where grief subsides, where changes are no more,
And life's tumultuous billows cease to roar;
She leaves her earthly mansion for the skies,
Where new creations feast her wond'ring eyes.

To heav'n's high mandate cheerfully resign'd
She mounts, and leaves the rolling globe behind;
She, who late wish'd that Leonard might return,
Has ceas'd to languish, and forgot to mourn;
To the same high empyreal mansions come,
She joins her spouse, and smiles upon the tomb:
And thus I hear her from the realms above:
"Lo! this the kingdom of celestial love!
"Could ye, fond parents, see our present bliss,
"How soon would you each sigh, each fear dismiss?
"Amidst unutter'd pleasures whilst I play
"In the fair sunshine of celestial day,
"As far as grief affects an happy soul
"So far doth grief my better mind controul,
"To see on earth my aged parents mourn,
"And secret wish for T——-! to return:
"Let brighter scenes your ev'ning-hours employ:
"Converse with heav'n, and taste the promis'd joy"

NIOBE IN DISTRESS FOR
HER CHILDREN SLAIN BY APOLLO

FROM OVID'S METAMORPHOSES,
BOOK VI. AND FROM A VIEW OF THE
PAINTING OF MR. RICHARD WILSON.

APOLLO's wrath to man the dreadful spring
Of ills innum'rous, tuneful goddess, sing!
Thou who did'st first th' ideal pencil give,
And taught'st the painter in his works to live,
Inspire with glowing energy of thought,
What Wilson painted, and what Ovid wrote.
Muse! lend thy aid, nor let me sue in vain,
Tho' last and meanest of the rhyming train!
O guide my pen in lofty strains to show
The Phrygian queen, all beautiful in woe.

  'Twas where Maeonia spreads her wide domain
Niobe dwelt, and held her potent reign:
See in her hand the regal sceptre shine,
The wealthy heir of Tantalus divine,
He most distinguish'd by Dodonean Jove,
To approach the tables of the gods above:
Her grandsire Atlas, who with mighty pains
Th' ethereal axis on his neck sustains:
Her other grandsire on the throne on high
Rolls the loud-pealing thunder thro' the sky.
Her spouse, Amphion, who from Jove too springs,
Divinely taught to sweep the sounding strings.

Seven sprightly sons the royal bed adorn,
Seven daughters beauteous as the op'ning morn,
As when Aurora fills the ravish'd sight,
And decks the orient realms with rosy light
From their bright eyes the living splendors play,
Nor can beholders bear the flashing ray.

Wherever, Niobe, thou turn'st thine eyes,
New beauties kindle, and new joys arise!
But thou had'st far the happier mother prov'd,
If this fair offspring had been less belov'd:
What if their charms exceed Aurora's teint.
No words could tell them, and no pencil paint,
Thy love too vehement hastens to destroy
Each blooming maid, and each celestial boy.

Now Manto comes, endu'd with mighty skill,
The past to explore, the future to reveal.
Thro' Thebes' wide streets Tiresia's daughter came,
Divine Latona's mandate to proclaim:
The Theban maids to hear the orders ran,
When thus Maeonia's prophetess began:

"Go, Thebans! great Latona's will obey,
"And pious tribute at her altars pay:
"With rights divine, the goddess be implor'd,
"Nor be her sacred offspring unador'd."
Thus Manto spoke. The Theban maids obey,
And pious tribute to the goddess pay.
The rich perfumes ascend in waving spires,
And altars blaze with consecrated fires;
The fair assembly moves with graceful air,
And leaves of laurel bind the flowing hair.

Niobe comes with all her royal race,
With charms unnumber'd, and superior grace:
Her Phrygian garments of delightful hue,
Inwove with gold, refulgent to the view,
Beyond description beautiful she moves
Like heav'nly Venus, 'midst her smiles and loves:
She views around the supplicating train,
And shakes her graceful head with stern disdain,
Proudly she turns around her lofty eyes,
And thus reviles celestial deities:
"What madness drives the Theban ladies fair
"To give their incense to surrounding air?
"Say why this new sprung deity preferr'd?
"Why vainly fancy your petitions heard?
"Or say why Caeus offspring is obey'd,
"While to my goddesship no tribute's paid?
"For me no altars blaze with living fires,
"No bullock bleeds, no frankincense transpires,
"Tho' Cadmus' palace, not unknown to fame,
"And Phrygian nations all revere my name.
"Where'er I turn my eyes vast wealth I find,
"Lo! here an empress with a goddess join'd.
"What, shall a Titaness be deify'd,
"To whom the spacious earth a couch deny'd!
"Nor heav'n, nor earth, nor sea receiv'd your queen,
"Till pitying Delos took the wand'rer in.
"Round me what a large progeny is spread!
"No frowns of fortune has my soul to dread.
"What if indignant she decrease my train
"More than Latona's number will remain;
"Then hence, ye Theban dames, hence haste away,
"Nor longer off'rings to Latona pay;
"Regard the orders of Amphion's spouse,
"And take the leaves of laurel from your brows."
Niobe spoke. The Theban maids obey'd,

Their brows unbound, and left the rights unpaid.
The angry goddess heard, then silence broke
On Cynthus' summit, and indignant spoke;
"Phoebus! behold, thy mother in disgrace,
"Who to no goddess yields the prior place
"Except to Juno's self, who reigns above,
"The spouse and sister of the thund'ring Jove.
"Niobe, sprung from Tantalus, inspires
"Each Theban bosom with rebellious fires;
"No reason her imperious temper quells,
"But all her father in her tongue rebels;
"Wrap her own sons for her blaspheming breath,
"Apollo! wrap them in the shades of death."
Latona ceas'd, and ardent thus replies
The God, whose glory decks th' expanded skies.
"Cease thy complaints, mine be the task assign'd
"To punish pride, and scourge the rebel mind."
This Phoebe join'd.—They wing their instant flight;
Thebes trembled as th' immortal pow'rs alight.
With clouds incompass'd glorious Phoebus stands;
The feather'd vengeance quiv'ring in his hands.

Near Cadmus' walls a plain extended lay,
Where Thebes' young princes pass'd in sport the day:
There the bold coursers bounded o'er the plains,
While their great masters held the golden reins.
Ismenus first the racing pastime led,
And rul'd the fury of his flying steed.
"Ah me," he sudden cries, with shrieking breath,
While in his breast he feels the shaft of death;
He drops the bridle on his courser's mane,
Before his eyes in shadows swims the plain,
He, the first-born of great Amphion's bed,
Was struck the first, first mingled with the dead.

Then didst thou, Sipylus, the language hear
Of fate portentous whistling in the air:
As when th' impending storm the sailor sees
He spreads his canvas to the fav'ring breeze,
So to thine horse thou gav'st the golden reins,
Gav'st him to rush impetuous o'er the plains:
But ah! a fatal shaft from Phoebus' hand
Smites thro' thy neck, and sinks thee on the sand.

Two other brothers were at wrestling found,
And in their pastime claspt each other round:
A shaft that instant from Apollo's hand
Transfixt them both, and stretcht them on the sand:
Together they their cruel fate bemoan'd,
Together languish'd, and together groan'd:
Together too th' unbodied spirits fled,
And sought the gloomy mansions of the dead.
Alphenor saw, and trembling at the view,
Beat his torn breast, that chang'd its snowy hue.
He flies to raise them in a kind embrace;
A brother's fondness triumphs in his face:
Alphenor fails in this fraternal deed,
A dart dispatch'd him (so the fates decreed:)
Soon as the arrow left the deadly wound,
His issuing entrails smoak'd upon the ground.
What woes on blooming Damasichon wait!
His sighs portend his near impending fate.
Just where the well-made leg begins to be,
And the soft sinews form the supple knee,
The youth sore wounded by the Delian god
Attempts t' extract the crime-avenging rod,
But, whilst he strives the will of fate t' avert,
Divine Apollo sends a second dart;
Swift thro' his throat the feather'd mischief flies,
Bereft of sense, he drops his head, and dies.

Young Ilioneus, the last, directs his pray'r,
And cries, "My life, ye gods celestial! spare."
Apollo heard, and pity touch'd his heart,
But ah! too late, for he had sent the dart:
Thou too, O Ilioneus, art doom'd to fall,
The fates refuse that arrow to recal.

On the swift wings of ever flying Fame
To Cadmus' palace soon the tidings came:
Niobe heard, and with indignant eyes
She thus express'd her anger and surprise:
"Why is such privilege to them allow'd?
"Why thus insulted by the Delian god?
"Dwells there such mischief in the pow'rs above?
"Why sleeps the vengeance of immortal Jove?"
For now Amphion too, with grief oppress'd,
Had plung'd the deadly dagger in his breast.
Niobe now, less haughty than before,
With lofty head directs her steps no more
She, who late told her pedigree divine,
And drove the Thebans from Latona's shrine,
How strangely chang'd!—yet beautiful in woe,
She weeps, nor weeps unpity'd by the foe.
On each pale corse the wretched mother spread
Lay overwhelm'd with grief, and kiss'd her dead,
Then rais'd her arms, and thus, in accents slow,
"Be sated cruel Goddess! with my woe;
"If I've offended, let these streaming eyes,
"And let this sev'nfold funeral suffice:
"Ah! take this wretched life you deign'd to save,
"With them I too am carried to the grave.
"Rejoice triumphant, my victorious foe,
"But show the cause from whence your triumphs flow?
"Tho' I unhappy mourn these children slain,
"Yet greater numbers to my lot remain."

She ceas'd, the bow string twang'd with awful sound,
Which struck with terror all th' assembly round,
Except the queen, who stood unmov'd alone,
By her distresses more presumptuous grown.
Near the pale corses stood their sisters fair
In sable vestures and dishevell'd hair;
One, while she draws the fatal shaft away,
Faints, falls, and sickens at the light of day.
To sooth her mother, lo! another flies,
And blames the fury of inclement skies,
And, while her words a filial pity show,
Struck dumb—indignant seeks the shades below.
Now from the fatal place another flies,
Falls in her flight, and languishes, and dies.
Another on her sister drops in death;
A fifth in trembling terrors yields her breath;
While the sixth seeks some gloomy cave in vain,
Struck with the rest, and mingled with the slain.

   One only daughter lives, and she the least;
The queen close clasp'd the daughter to her breast:
"Ye heav'nly pow'rs, ah spare me one," she cry'd,
"Ah! spare me one," the vocal hills reply'd:
In vain she begs, the Fates her suit deny,
In her embrace she sees her daughter die.

   "The queen of all her family bereft,[8]
"Without or husband, son, or daughter left,
"Grew stupid at the shock. The passing air
"Made no impression on her stiff'ning hair.
"The blood forsook her face: amidst the flood
"Pour'd from her cheeks, quite fix'd her eye-balls
"stood.

---

8   This verse to the end is the work of another hand.

"Her tongue, her palate both obdurate grew,
"Her curdled veins no longer motion knew;
"The use of neck, and arms, and feet was gone,
"And ev'n her bowels hard'ned into stone:
"A marble statue now the queen appears,
"But from the marble steal the silent tears."

TO S. M.
A YOUNG AFRICAN PAINTER,
ON SEEING HIS WORKS

TO show the lab'ring bosom's deep intent,
And thought in living characters to paint,
When first thy pencil did those beauties give,
And breathing figures learnt from thee to live,
How did those prospects give my soul delight,
A new creation rushing on my sight?
Still, wond'rous youth! each noble path pursue,
On deathless glories fix thine ardent view:
Still may the painter's and the poet's fire
To aid thy pencil, and thy verse conspire!
And may the charms of each seraphic theme
Conduct thy footsteps to immortal fame!
High to the blissful wonders of the skies
Elate thy soul, and raise thy wishful eyes.
Thrice happy, when exalted to survey
That splendid city, crown'd with endless day,
Whose twice six gates on radiant hinges ring:
Celestial Salem blooms in endless spring.

Calm and serene thy moments glide along,
And may the muse inspire each future song!
Still, with the sweets of contemplation bless'd,
May peace with balmy wings your soul invest!
But when these shades of time are chas'd away,
And darkness ends in everlasting day,
On what seraphic pinions shall we move,
And view the landscapes in the realms above?

There shall thy tongue in heav'nly murmurs flow,
And there my muse with heav'nly transport glow:
No more to tell of Damon's tender sighs,
Or rising radiance of Aurora's eyes,
For nobler themes demand a nobler strain,
And purer language on th' ethereal plain.
Cease, gentle muse! the solemn gloom of night
Now seals the fair creation from my sight.

TO HIS HONOUR THE LIEUTENANT-GOVERNOR

ON THE DEATH OF HIS LADY.
MARCH 24, 1773

ALL-Conquering Death! by thy resistless pow'r,
Hope's tow'ring plumage falls to rise no more!
Of scenes terrestrial how the glories fly,
Forget their splendors, and submit to die!
Who ere escap'd thee, but the saint[9] of old
Beyond the flood in sacred annals told,
And the great sage[10] whom fiery coursers drew
To heav'n's bright portals from Elisha's view;
Wond'ring he gaz'd at the refulgent car,
Then snatch'd the mantle floating on the air.
From Death these only could exemption boast,
And without dying gain'd th' immortal coast.
Not falling millions sate the tyrant's mind,
Nor can the victor's progress be confin'd.
But cease thy strife with Death, fond Nature, cease:
He leads the virtuous to the realms of peace;
His to conduct to the immortal plains,
Where heav'n's Supreme in bliss and glory reigns.

---

9   Enoch.

10   Elijah.

There sits, illustrious Sir, thy beauteous spouse;
A gem-blaz'd circle beaming on her brows.
Hail'd with acclaim among the heav'nly choirs,
Her soul new-kindling with seraphic fires,
To notes divine she tunes the vocal strings,
While heav'n's high concave with the music rings.
Virtue's rewards can mortal pencil paint?
No—all descriptive arts, and eloquence are faint;
Nor canst thou, Oliver, assent refuse
To heav'nly tidings from the Afric muse.

As soon may change thy laws, eternal fate,
As the saint miss the glories I relate;
Or her Benevolence forgotten lie,
Which wip'd the trick'ling tear from Misry's eye.
Whene'er the adverse winds were known to blow,
When loss to loss * ensu'd, and woe to woe,
Calm and serene beneath her father's hand
She sat resign'd to the divine command.

No longer then, great Sir, her death deplore,
And let us hear the mournful sigh no more,
Restrain the sorrow streaming from thine eye,
Be all thy future moments crown'd with joy!
Nor let thy wishes be to earth confin'd,
But soaring high pursue th' unbodied mind.
Forgive the muse, forgive th' advent'rous lays,
That fain thy soul to heav'nly scenes would raise.

A FAREWEL TO AMERICA. TO MRS. S. W.

I

ADIEU, New-England's smiling meads,
  Adieu, the flow'ry plain:
I leave thine op'ning charms, O spring,
  And tempt the roaring main.

II

In vain for me the flow'rets rise,
  And boast their gaudy pride,
While here beneath the northern skies
  I mourn for health deny'd.

III

Celestial maid of rosy hue,
  O let me feel thy reign!
I languish till thy face I view,
  Thy vanish'd joys regain.

IV

Susanna mourns, nor can I bear
   To see the crystal show'r,
Or mark the tender falling tear
   At sad departure's hour;

V

Not unregarding can I see
   Her soul with grief opprest:
But let no sighs, no groans for me,
   Steal from her pensive breast.

VI

In vain the feather'd warblers sing,
   In vain the garden blooms,
And on the bosom of the spring
   Breathes out her sweet perfumes.

VII

While for Britannia's distant shore
   We sweep the liquid plain,
And with astonish'd eyes explore
   The wide-extended main.

VIII

Lo! Health appears! celestial dame!
   Complacent and serene,
With Hebe's mantle o'er her Frame,
   With soul-delighting mein.

IX

To mark the vale where London lies
   With misty vapours crown'd,
Which cloud Aurora's thousand dyes,
   And veil her charms around.

X

Why, Phoebus, moves thy car so slow?
   So slow thy rising ray?
Give us the famous town to view,
   Thou glorious king of day!

XI

For thee, Britannia, I resign
   New-England's smiling fields;
To view again her charms divine,
   What joy the prospect yields!

XII

But thou! Temptation hence away,
    With all thy fatal train,
Nor once seduce my soul away,
    By thine enchanting strain.

XIII

Thrice happy they, whose heav'nly shield
    Secures their souls from harms,
And fell Temptation on the field
    Of all its pow'r disarms!

BOSTON,
May 7, 1773.

A REBUS, BY I. B.

_____

I

A BIRD delicious to the taste,
On which an army once did feast,
  Sent by an hand unseen;
A creature of the horned race,
Which Britain's royal standards grace;
  A gem of vivid green;

II

A town of gaiety and sport,
Where beaux and beauteous nymphs resort,
  And gallantry doth reign;
A Dardan hero fam'd of old
For youth and beauty, as we're told,
  And by a monarch slain;

III

A peer of popular applause,
Who doth our violated laws,
  And grievances proclaim.
Th' initials show a vanquish'd town,
That adds fresh glory and renown
  To old Britannia's fame.

AN ANSWER TO THE REBUS, BY THE AUTHOR OF THESE POEMS

THE poet asks, and Phillis can't refuse
To show th' obedience of the Infant muse.
She knows the Quail of most inviting taste
Fed Israel's army in the dreary waste;
And what's on Britain's royal standard borne,
But the tall, graceful, rampant Unicorn?
The Emerald with a vivid verdure glows
Among the gems which regal crowns compose;
Boston's a town, polite and debonair,
To which the beaux and beauteous nymphs repair,
Each Helen strikes the mind with sweet surprise,
While living lightning flashes from her eyes,
See young Euphorbus of the Dardan line
By Manelaus' hand to death resign:
The well known peer of popular applause
Is C——m zealous to support our laws.
Quebec now vanquish'd must obey,
She too much annual tribute pay
To Britain of immortal fame.
And add new glory to her name.

Made in the USA
Las Vegas, NV
03 March 2023

68498445R00080